# Prerequisites for Fundraising Success:

*18 Things Every Fundraising Professional, Board Member, or Volunteer Needs to Know*

Melvin B. Shaw, M.A.Ed.
Pearl D. Shaw, M.P.A., C.F.R.E.

First printing - January 2013
Printed in the United States of America

This book is dedicated to the men, women and young people who commit their time, resources and talents to the nonprofit organizations, institutions and associations they believe in. Thank you for taking the time to make this world a better place.

Thanks to all our clients who trust us to provide guidance as they grow their fundraising programs and campaigns.

Special thanks to Jill Keith, Sara Henneberger, Lynn Nguyen and Eddie Tucker for their work in bringing this book to life.

# Table of Contents

# Introduction

Sustained, successful fundraising requires consistent attention, action, funding, and leadership. It is proactive and volunteer-driven. The success of an organization's or institution's fundraising depends upon the involvement of board members — specifically, their ability and willingness to cultivate and solicit major donors. This is where it all begins. If the leadership of an organization is not behind a fundraising initiative, it will be very difficult for volunteers or staff to experience success.

This book shares the 18 prerequisites for fundraising success that we have identified through our extensive experience working with non-profit organizations and institutions. Good intentions, desire, and commitment abound amongst board members, staff, and volunteers. While these traits are a mandatory prerequisite for fundraising success, they are not enough.

You will also need board members, volunteer leadership, and staff who have access to individuals and institutions that can provide the financial and other resources you seek to secure. You will need strong project management skills and the ability to ensure that your fundraising goals remain a priority in spite of other emerging and/or unpredicted priorities. Volunteer recruitment and management will be key to your success. So will creativity, strategic thinking, and the ability to take advantage of opportunities as they arise.

Always keep in mind that successful fundraising is donor focused. While it may sound counterintuitive, fundraising is not necessarily about you and your organization or institution. Success comes when you understand why your current and potential donors want to support your organization and when you value those motivations. When donor motivations are valued, the nature of the relationship between a donor and an institution can transform from one where donors are viewed primarily as a revenue source to one where donors and institutions partner to achieve a common goal.

A vital component of sustained success is the development of a mutually beneficial relationship between an organization and its supporters. This starts by consistently honoring and rewarding the efforts of donors and volunteers. When benefits are offered that meet identified donor needs as well as those that are unarticulated, you will enhance the lives and aspirations of your supporters while sowing the seeds for their continued involvement.

# A Word About Language

We have written this book as a way of sharing with you what we have learned over many years. Our vision is that you will use it as you work with those organizations and institutions that you believe in. You may be engaged as a volunteer, as a member of the development staff, or as the CEO, president, or executive officer. You may be working with a local non-profit organization or with a national advocacy group, or perhaps you are raising money for a hospital, museum, or educational institution. While we recognize that there are differences of scale, governance, and capacity, we also know that the fundraising principles and techniques that we share are effective across these differences.

Throughout this book we use the words organization and institution interchangeably. Sometimes we use both words. Sometimes we use the phrase executive director and sometimes we use the word president. Other times we use the phrase chief executive officer. We do so in order to be inclusive and to reflect the different titles in use. In regard to gender, sometimes we use the word he and other times we use she. Our hope is that as you work through this book, you will read yourself and your fundraising activities into the words.

We seek to be inclusive, for fundraising — and the non-profit sector in general — is truly dependent upon the goodwill of a cross section of individuals who believe in the mission and vision of the organizations and institutions with which they work.

Finally, we want you to use this book. Please write in the margins and circle ideas you wish to share with others. Don't worry about marking up the checklists contained within each chapter; we have included extra copies at the end for you and for others you feel would benefit from these exercises.

*Thank you for taking the time to help create the world you want to live in!*

# Getting Started — Prerequisites for Fundraising Success

We offer the ideas contained within this book as a guide to help you reach your fundraising goals. Our experience has shown that fundraising success can be predicted by the extent to which an organization or institution has implemented and embraced the following 18 prerequisites for success. The following table provides a summary of these prerequisites.

We suggest that you review the table with an eye to the organization or institution you are most closely identified with. Think about what you know — and what you don't know. Based on your current understanding and involvement, take a moment to indicate whether or not you believe the prerequisite is *present* or *yet to be developed*. If you are not sure, place a mark in the *not sure* column.

| PREREQUISITES | |
|---|---|
| ☐ Present<br>☐ To be Developed<br>☐ Not Sure | Attain full understanding and agreement regarding the organization's mission, vision, goals, strategic direction, and financial position amongst the organization's leadership. |
| | Comments: |
| ☐ Present<br>☐ To be Developed<br>☐ Not Sure | Achieve full commitment from the board of directors, CEO, executive director or president, and top fundraising staff. |
| | Comments: |
| ☐ Present<br>☐ To be Developed<br>☐ Not Sure | Develop an active fundraising leadership team that meets regularly. |
| | Comments: |
| ☐ Present<br>☐ To be Developed<br>☐ Not Sure | Allocate funds and resources required for implementation of the fundraising plan. |
| | Comments: |

| | PREREQUISITES |
|---|---|
| ☐ Present<br>☐ To be<br>   Developed<br>☐ Not Sure | Create a clear, concise, and compelling case for financial support that ties back to the organization's strategic plan. |
| | Comments: |
| ☐ Present<br>☐ To be<br>   Developed<br>☐ Not Sure | Complete a fundraising assessment and feasibility study or survey. |
| | Comments: |
| ☐ Present<br>☐ To be<br>   Developed<br>☐ Not Sure | Develop a time-phased fundraising plan. |
| | Comments: |
| ☐ Present<br>☐ To be<br>   Developed<br>☐ Not Sure | Define roles and responsibilities for staff, board members, volunteers, and consultants. |
| | Comments: |
| ☐ Present<br>☐ To be<br>   Developed<br>☐ Not Sure | Hire professional staff whose primary role is fundraising management, volunteer training and management, and administrative support. |
| | Comments: |
| ☐ Present<br>☐ To be<br>   Developed<br>☐ Not Sure | Identify top-caliber volunteer leadership. |
| | Comments: |
| ☐ Present<br>☐ To be<br>   Developed<br>☐ Not Sure | Craft fundraising guidelines, policies, and procedures. |
| | Comments: |
| ☐ Present<br>☐ To be<br>   Developed<br>☐ Not Sure | Recruit a team of properly trained and informed volunteers. |
| | Comments: |

| | **PREREQUISITES** |
|---|---|
| ☐ Present<br>☐ To be<br>Developed<br>☐ Not Sure | Use a donor database system to facilitate fundraising management and decision making. |
| | Comments: |
| ☐ Present<br>☐ To be<br>Developed<br>☐ Not Sure | Coordinate solicitation strategies. |
| | Comments: |
| ☐ Present<br>☐ To be<br>Developed<br>☐ Not Sure | Create a strong awareness and education program to complement and support fundraising activities. |
| | Comments: |
| ☐ Present<br>☐ To be<br>Developed<br>☐ Not Sure | Thank and recognize donors and volunteers. |
| | Comments: |
| ☐ Present<br>☐ To be<br>Developed<br>☐ Not Sure | Offer meaningful donor benefit packages and naming opportunities. |
| | Comments: |
| ☐ Present<br>☐ To be<br>Developed<br>☐ Not Sure | Encourage open lines of communication amongst all parties, combined with a sense of urgency. |
| | Comments: |

Each of these is described in detail in the remainder of this book. Although some are discussed more thoroughly due to their pivotal role, each plays an important part in advancing your fundraising success.

As you progress through this book, take a moment to return to this checklist to review your initial assessment. If your assessment has changed, consider what has led you to alter your perspective. Think about those ideas you have absorbed that you may want to share with board members, staff, or volunteers. Write in the margins and circle the items you want to remember. Use the checklists at the end of each chapter. Fill in the sections we have designed for your notes. We have written this book for you to use.

CHAPTER 1

# Building Consensus

**Agreement**

*Attain full understanding and agreement regarding the organization's mission, vision, goals, strategic direction, and financial position amongst the organization's leadership.*

Successful fundraising begins long before a fundraising plan is ever created. It starts with your organization's vision and mission. These two items are at the core of non-profit operations. It is the vision and mission that drive your strategic direction and goals. And it is the strategic direction that influences fundraising and the use of funds.

The chief executive for your organization is the person responsible for the vision and mission. He is responsible for ensuring board members, employees, and volunteers understand the mission and vision and are in agreement with these. He is also responsible for ensuring the organization's strategic direction — as documented in the strategic plan — are rooted in the mission and vision.

Your vision statement communicates your vision for the future — what you are seeking to achieve. Your mission statement communicates the purpose of your organization. Your strategic plan communicates how you will bring your vision and mission to life.

Your vision and mission statements should be short and concise — one or two sentences at most, if possible. Your strategic plan can be as simple or as complex as your organization requires. We are partial to short, clearly written plans that include easy-to-understand and easy-to-measure goals and objectives.

Once the vision and mission are established, it is the chief executive's responsibility to ensure they are understood and that the board and employees are in agreement with them. He needs to know these statements inside and out, and be able to discuss the vision and mission whenever he talks about the organization. He needs to know the goals and objectives contained in the strategic plan and the progress being made toward these.

Sometimes we find that the vision, mission, and strategic directions are documented, but that they exist primarily on paper. Discussing these helps bring them back into focus and allows for consensus — or dissenting viewpoints — to develop.

If you find it is challenging to secure understanding and agreement, don't worry — it is better to know now rather than later. Agreement is something that needs to be retained over the years, and sometimes things change. For example, it may be that new board members or employees joined the organization and did not participate in an orientation session that communicated these themes. Or, it may be that the needs of the community have changed, and the vision and mission need to be updated. You may have achieved the goals of your last strategic plan but have not yet created a new one. These are good things to know — and to take action on.

If your vision, mission, and strategic plan need revising, take the time to do so. This may require the assistance of a strategic planning consultant so that all parties can participate fully in the brainstorming and planning processes. If it does, it is worth the investment: working from a plan helps ensure that resources are used effectively and that all members of the organization are working in concert toward agreed upon goals.

We place a lot of emphasis on the vision, mission, and strategic plan because they are the starting point for your fundraising. When you begin discussions on how much money your organization needs to raise, you will want to refer to your strategic plan to map out what you are seeking to achieve over the coming years. From there you can begin to map out costs and fundraising goals.

As you read through this book you will become familiar with the phrase "case for support." This refers to a document that will be at the heart of your fundraising. It communicates what you are seeking to achieve, how much it will cost, and what the impact of your work will be. All of these should be drawn from your strategic plan, which should be rooted in your vision and mission.

When the leadership of your organization fully understands your vision and mission, they are in a strong position to evaluate — and, as necessary, modify — the strategic plan. Understanding the strategic plan allows leaders — executives and board members — to make informed financial projections. Understanding the organization's financial position and projections informs fundraising and assures that the organization is engaged in proactive fundraising instead of "emergency fundraising."

Consistent monitoring and assessment of financial statements helps support organizational stability and growth. Take the time to ensure board members understand the implications of the financials they are asked to review. Encourage open discussion and questions regarding the organization's financial position. Discuss the variables that could impact your organization's financial position for better or for worse. Ensure that plans are put in place to address these possibilities should they arise. Review the size of your reserve fund and what expenses it could cover. If your organization doesn't have a reserve fund, put plans in place to create and grow one. A reserve fund provides options for addressing an unanticipated increase in demand for services or a decrease in revenue.

The economy may change without notice, and donors and funders may change their giving priorities — situations beyond anyone's control. But they do not need to jeopardize an organization's financial health. Implementing the prerequisites for fundraising success laid out in this book will help build the fundraising capacity and infrastructure you will need to respond to changes in the market.

Your organization's vision, mission, and strategic plan will play a key role in determining your fundraising success. When combined with an understanding of the organization's financial position, they comprise the first prerequisite for fundraising success. Take the time you need to ensure these are in place, up to date, and that there is full understanding and agreement amongst the organization's leadership.

# Understanding and Agreement Checklist

The following is a sample checklist you can use as you go through the process of building understanding and agreement in regard to your organization's vision, mission, strategic plan, and financial position. Review each item and mark whether or not it applies to your organization. If you are not sure, indicate that.

| APPLIES TO YOUR ORGANIZATION | DESCRIPTION |
| --- | --- |
| ☐ Yes ☐ No ☐ Not Sure | Our documented vision and mission statements reflect our vision and mission. |
| | Comments: |
| ☐ Yes ☐ No ☐ Not Sure | All members of the board understand and agree with our vision and mission statements. |
| | Comments: |
| ☐ Yes ☐ No ☐ Not Sure | Our strategic plan brings our mission and vision to life. |
| | Comments: |
| ☐ Yes ☐ No ☐ Not Sure | Our strategic plan is up to date. |
| | Comments: |
| ☐ Yes ☐ No ☐ Not Sure | Our strategic plan includes time frames and measurable goals. |
| | Comments: |
| ☐ Yes ☐ No ☐ Not Sure | All members of the board understand and agree with our strategic plan. |
| | Comments: |

| APPLIES TO YOUR ORGANIZATION | DESCRIPTION |
|---|---|
| ☐ Yes ☐ No ☐ Not Sure | We use our strategic plan as part of our ongoing program planning and evaluation. |
| | Comments: |
| ☐ Yes ☐ No ☐ Not Sure | We refer to our strategic plan when making funding and personnel decisions. |
| | Comments: |
| ☐ Yes ☐ No ☐ Not Sure | Our leadership understands the organization's current financial position. |
| | Comments: |
| ☐ Yes ☐ No ☐ Not Sure | We monitor and assess our financials on a regular basis, making adjustments as needed. |
| | Comments: |
| ☐ Yes ☐ No ☐ Not Sure | We have plans in place for how to address increased demand for services or reductions in funding. |
| | Comments: |

## What Next?

Has your organization achieved all or most of the items on this list? Congratulations! You have built the first layer of a firm foundation from which to develop and grow your fundraising activities. As you move forward, never lose sight of your organization's key values and financial position, for they will help inform all future decisions.

Is your organization struggling with many of the above items, or are you not sure of their status? Now is the time, before pursuing any further development activities, to address problems or uncertainty regarding your organization's values, mission, strategic plan, and financial standing. Investigate the areas of weakness you have identified via the checklist. Who in the organization is responsible for addressing these issues? When and how can they work together to overcome them? What logistical or philosophical barriers need to be discussed? What resources are needed? What is a reasonable timeline for successfully completing this checklist? We encourage you to invest the time and effort to reach full understanding and agreement — your organization's sustained success depends on it.

**Notes:**_____

_____

_____

**Three Actions I Will Take:**

1. _____

2. _____

3. _____

CHAPTER 2

# Committing to the Cause

*Achieve full commitment from the board of directors, the CEO, executive director or president, and top fundraising staff.*

The full commitment of the board of directors, CEO, staff, and volunteer leadership is *key* to fundraising success. Without this commitment, it is next to impossible to meet fundraising goals. People who are committed embody the following characteristics. They:

1. Understand how much money the organization is seeking to raise and what the funds will be used for
2. Understand the impact the organization makes, why it is important, and how it is different from other organizations
3. Understand the organization's strategic plan and how the proposed fundraising initiative ties to the strategic plan
4. Believe the fundraising goal is achievable
5. Believe in the leadership of the organization, its integrity, and its accountability
6. Make their own financial gift and ask others to do so
7. Understand where the projected revenue will come from and what plans are in place if initial solicitations are not successful
8. Generate enthusiasm for fundraising and encourage others to join them
9. Come prepared to meetings and remain in contact with other members of the organization's leadership and fundraising team between meetings

10. Help secure in-kind resources that can offset organizational or fundraising costs
11. Share their creativity, resources, and problem solving skills to help advance fundraising
12. Follow through on agreements and assignments

While it may take time to cultivate and secure the full commitment of an organization's key stakeholders, this step cannot be pushed aside. If a fundraising initiative is the vision of the executive director, this person should take the time to meet individually with board members and share with them her vision and commitment. The executive director will need to let the board members know what it will take to make the vision a reality and *ask for their support*. At these meetings, the executive director should be prepared to answer questions and overcome objections.

Likewise, if a project is the vision of the board of directors, the board chair should take the time to meet personally with the executive director to share the board's vision and explain how the project will advance the organization's mission and strategic plan. The board should be prepared to answer the executive director's questions and to provide her with the resources, support, and leadership that the proposed fundraising initiative will require.

**Note:** The questions and objections raised by board members or the executive director may not be different from those that will need to be overcome when talking with prospective donors and partners. These comments, questions, and/or objectives can be most helpful in developing the initiative's "case for support," discussed later in chapter five.

Regardless of where a project originates, all leaders within the organization will need to be engaged in the process of defining the fundraising project and its financial goals. **All leaders need to be included from the beginning.** Their commitment and engagement is what will help secure funds, involvement, partnerships, and in-kind resources.

After initial individual conversations have occurred, it will be important to dedicate time during board meetings to discuss the proposed fundraising initiative in depth. This should be a conversation that invites board members to grapple with the proposed fundraising initiative, ask questions, raise doubts, share strategies and ideas, and express enthusiasm. An open discussion — and the allocation of enough time for a full discussion — is important. It may be appropriate to schedule a retreat dedicated to the topic of fundraising. Many organizations have such retreats once a year. Others will host a retreat when planning for a capital campaign or other fundraising initiative of special significance.

Always leave enough time for all parties to fully understand and commit to a proposed fundraising goal. **This is the most important prerequisite —** without full commitment, there is a greater potential for fundraising challenges.

## Think Big — Expand Your Definition Of Leadership

In addition to formally recognized leadership such as an executive director, president, development director, or board chair, it is important to gain the support of your organization's informal leadership — those stakeholders who have supported your organization over the years with their time, money, and talent. Ideally you will talk with your major donors, your most consistent donors, and your volunteers, consultants, and staff as you develop your fundraising initiative. Remember, fundraising requires more than money. Talking with your extended or informal leadership will help you engage the best thinking, involvement, creativity, and networks of those closest to your organization. These individuals can provide ideas and resources that extend beyond those you thought of originally.

Another thing to remember is that prospective donors and funders always ask about the involvement of key stakeholders, particularly board members. In fact, many will shy away from initiatives that do not have demonstrated internal commitment and engagement. For example, many foundations explicitly ask about board giving. They want to know the percentage of board members who give, total dollars contributed, and funds raised through the efforts of board members. The feeling is, "If those closest to you don't support the project, why should we?" For educational institutions, there is a focus on the rate of alumni giving, the retention of alumni donors, and total funds contributed by alumni.

Take the time to engage your leadership before approaching people outside the organization. Make sure you secure financial gifts and in-kind resources from your leadership and top donors before you solicit others.

# Commitment Checklist

The following is a sample checklist you can use as you go through the process of securing the full commitment of your organization's leadership. Review each item and mark whether or not it applies to your organization. If you are not sure, indicate that.

| APPLIES TO YOUR ORGANIZATION | DESCRIPTION |
| --- | --- |
| ☐ Yes<br>☐ No<br>☐ Not Sure | Time is allocated for the board, staff, and top leadership to discuss proposed fundraising initiatives before they are publicly announced.<br>Comments: |
| ☐ Yes<br>☐ No<br>☐ Not Sure | Input is sought from leaders across the organization including major donors, long-term volunteers, and informal leaders.<br>Comments: |
| ☐ Yes<br>☐ No<br>☐ Not Sure | Board chair agrees with fundraising priorities and financial goals and believes they are achievable.<br>Comments: |
| ☐ Yes<br>☐ No<br>☐ Not Sure | Board membership agrees with fundraising priorities and financial goals and believes they are achievable.<br>Comments: |
| ☐ Yes<br>☐ No<br>☐ Not Sure | Executive director agrees with fundraising priorities and financial goals and believes they are achievable.<br>Comments: |
| ☐ Yes<br>☐ No<br>☐ Not Sure | Development/fundraising staff agrees with fundraising priorities and financial goals and believes they are achievable.<br>Comments: |

| APPLIES TO YOUR ORGANIZATION | DESCRIPTION |
|---|---|
| ☐ Yes ☐ No ☐ Not Sure | Board chair is willing to take an active role in guiding fundraising activities. |
| | Comments: |
| ☐ Yes ☐ No ☐ Not Sure | Board members, leadership-level volunteers, and organization's management are each willing to make a meaningful financial gift and to ask others to do so. |
| | Comments: |
| ☐ Yes ☐ No ☐ Not Sure | Executive director is willing to allocate the time required to work with development staff, cultivate and solicit donors, and participate in fundraising-related events and communications. |
| | Comments: |
| ☐ Yes ☐ No ☐ Not Sure | All staff members, consultants, and volunteers are willing to integrate promotion of fundraising into their activities. |
| | Comments: |
| ☐ Yes ☐ No ☐ Not Sure | All parties understand how much money the organization is seeking to raise and what the funds will be used for. |
| | Comments: |
| ☐ Yes ☐ No ☐ Not Sure | Board members, staff, and volunteers understand the organization's strategic plan and how the proposed fundraising initiative ties to the strategic plan. |
| | Comments: |
| ☐ Yes ☐ No ☐ Not Sure | Organization's leaders share their creativity, resources, and problem solving skills to help advance the initiative. |
| | Comments: |

## What Next?

If you answered yes to many or all of the above items, your organizational leadership is strong, engaged, and committed. Be proud of this accomplishment, and strive to maintain it through close communication and transparency in the future. As priorities or external factors shift and change, leaders and top fundraising staff should be prepared to actively assess their roles, discuss concerns, and recommit to the organization's direction and activities.

Is your organization lacking top-level support, or are the commitment levels of key players unknown or under-communicated? This is a challenge that must be addressed promptly and thoroughly. Consider whether your organizational culture discourages full commitment. Or perhaps expectations for performance and involvement have never been expressed clearly. A variety of tactics for improvement can be employed, whether it's a long-overdue conversation, a reassessment of job duties, an update to institutional policies, or changes in staffing. Remember, commitment — in words and actions — is the most important prerequisite for success.

**Notes:**_____

_____

_____

**Three Actions I Will Take:**

1. _____

2. _____

3. _____

# CHAPTER 3

# Teamwork Among Leaders

***Develop an active fundraising team that meets regularly.***

Fundraising is most effective when managed by a fundraising leadership team. Creating such a team will bring together those individuals (employees, board members, and volunteers) who are responsible for major components of your fundraising. They should meet on a regular basis to report on their progress and challenges. Members should work collaboratively to help your organization reach its fundraising goal. They should be empowered to make decisions, and the decisions made by this team should be respected and implemented by fundraising volunteers and employees.

A fundraising leadership team helps create accountability and transparency. Members are accountable to each other. Each member knows the commitments, roles, and responsibilities of all other members. There are no secrets. If there is a lull in gifts received, the full team knows about it. When new gifts are received, members know about it. When fundraising management reports are shared at each meeting, team members can monitor the progress of fundraising activities, ask pertinent questions, and work with each other to create new strategies and work-arounds.

With a strong fundraising leadership team, the actions of staff, board members, and volunteers are open to review by team members. Financial progress and expenses are reported regularly at these meetings. Members have the opportunity to share information and coordinate their activities for the benefit of the initiative.

When you have engaged qualified volunteers to assist with fundraising, you will be amazed at the solutions they can come up with. *The key to an effective fundraising leadership team is for it to be volunteer-led with support from staff.* That means the fundraising chair leads the team meetings, not the executive director or the chief development officer. It means that staff support the work of the fundraising chair by producing and distributing fundraising reports and taking and quickly distributing minutes that accurately capture action items and next steps. If you have selected a qualified fundraising chair and clearly defined his responsibilities, you will be amazed how he can assist you in meeting your fundraising goals. He will be able to do this because he has made them his goals. He is no longer helping your organization; he is now orchestrating and attracting people and resources for something he believes in.

> If your organization has a development committee of the board, we suggest that the chair of the development committee serve as a member of the fundraising leadership team.

The leadership team sets the tone, policy, and direction of your fundraising and monitors its progress. The committee should be led by the chair or co-chairs. These volunteers should be supported by the institution's chief development officer and the executive director.

Other potential members for this committee include:
1. Chair of the development committee of the board (if such a committee exists)
2. Board members
3. Major donors
4. Community and business leaders
5. Key stakeholders
6. Executive director or chief executive officer
7. Development director or chief fundraising officer
8. Finance director
9. Program staff
10. Employees with strong community ties

11. Chairs of each fundraising division
12. Top staff responsible for raising funds from specific sources

The following is an example of an agenda for a leadership team meeting.

| SAMPLE LEADERSHIP TEAM AGENDA | |
|---|---|
| 1. Welcome and opening remarks | Campaign co-chairs |
| 2. Introduction of new members | |
| 3. Review and approval of minutes from prior meeting | |
| 4. Special announcements, directives, and upcoming campaign activities | |
| 5. Report on campaign funds raised to date and since last meeting | Development director and finance director |
| 6. Reports from division chairs and campaign committees | Division and committee chairs with support from development staff |
|    a. Prospective donors identified | |
|    b. Unique solicitations | |
| 7. Funds raised to date and since last meeting (by division) | |
| 8. Resources and support needed | Campaign co-chairs and development staff |
| 9. Review and adjustment of items pending or incomplete | Campaign co-chairs |
| 10. Review of timeline and activity chart | Campaign co-chairs |
| 11. Determine which activities will be completed by when and by whom | Campaign co-chairs |
| 12. Other business | All |
| 13. Meeting summary and closing | Campaign co-chairs |

# Fundraising Leadership Team Checklist

The following checklist is provided to help you manage the process of recruiting your fundraising leaders.

| APPLIES TO YOUR ORGANIZATION | DESCRIPTION |
|---|---|
| ☐ Yes<br>☐ No<br>☐ Not Sure | Our chair takes the lead, ensures we meet monthly, requests reports, and follows up with members prior to the meeting to make sure they are prepared and have fulfilled their commitments. |
| | Comments: |
| ☐ Yes<br>☐ No<br>☐ Not Sure | Our volunteers recognize the importance of team meetings. They arrive on time, are prepared with information to report, fulfill their responsibilities in a timely fashion, and help contribute solutions when challenges arise. |
| | Comments: |
| ☐ Yes<br>☐ No<br>☐ Not Sure | Our staff produce timely and accurate fundraising reports for use by volunteers and employees. Data is up to date. Reports are easy to read and the format is consistent from month to month. |
| | Comments: |
| ☐ Yes<br>☐ No<br>☐ Not Sure | Team members provide updates on activities by other volunteers and staff. |
| | Comments: |
| ☐ Yes<br>☐ No<br>☐ Not Sure | Our meetings start on time and end on time. |
| | Comments: |

| APPLIES TO YOUR ORGANIZATION | DESCRIPTION |
|---|---|
| ☐ Yes<br>☐ No<br>☐ Not Sure | We use technology to help facilitate communication and participation. |
| | Comments: |
| ☐ Yes<br>☐ No<br>☐ Not Sure | Our minutes accurately reflect our work, decisions, and next steps. They are distributed within 24 hours of each meeting. |
| | Comments: |

# Tip

What is the common thread among the above items? Communication! From fundraising reports, to meeting minutes, to job descriptions, timely and accurate communication is at the heart of any successful leadership team. Members are aware of their responsibilities and those of their colleagues. They are well equipped with relevant information as they pursue their tasks. They engage with one another across mediums, always armed with the appropriate data. Importantly, they leave an accessible trail of information that can be utilized for future fundraising efforts.

Formalizing your communication process through the tasks on this checklist will streamline your team's efforts and help ensure the effective use of members' valuable time. Depending on the expertise of your leadership team and staff, it may help to provide templates for memos, minutes, and other written reports, along with basic guidelines for clear and concise communication.

**Notes:**_____

_____

_____


**Three Actions I Will Take:**

1. _____

2. _____

3. _____

# CHAPTER 4

# Funding Your Fundraising

**Resources**

*Allocate funds and resources required for implementation of the fundraising plan.*

Penny-wise and pound-foolish — or, what you put in is what you get back!

We have found that too many organizations have great visions, missions, and ideas but do not have the funds (or do not invest the funds) required to develop, launch, and sustain a fundraising initiative.

Another great saying that is echoed in our industry is, "It takes money to raise money." This is important to keep in mind if you want to operate at the highest and most productive levels. There are no shortcuts to launching a successful fundraising program. You will need funding or resources for some of the basics, such as:

1. Qualified staff
2. Data management technology
3. Marketing materials
4. Printing and publications
5. Postage
6. Website development and maintenance
7. Office space and equipment
8. Graphics
9. Copywriting

10. Funder and donor research
11. Grant writing

You will not be considered a serious player by volunteers or donors if you are not able to provide the basics required to develop and maintain a fundraising initiative. Think hard and long before you launch your fundraising. Make sure that you have allocated the financial and human resources you will need to sustain your fundraising and the relationships you develop. Unfortunately, there is a tendency amongst organizations to invest the least in areas like fundraising that result in the most, such as keeping the doors open!

A successful fundraising endeavor requires an investment of time, resources, and money. Put another way, *it takes money to raise money.* There is no way around it. That being said, small organizations should not feel defeated. Individuals and organizations that are closest to you can be sources of initial seed money. Start from where you are. Work to implement the prerequisites outlined in this book and you will find that you can attract the resources and people you need to meet your fundraising goals.

All prospective funders will want to see a budget. They will want to know what resources will be required to support your fundraising efforts. Your fundraising budget should be realistic, created in advance, and updated on a quarterly basis. It should include projected revenue and expenses.

Projected revenue should itemize sources with projected amounts, such as:
1. Direct mail
2. Earned revenue
3. Foundation grants
4. Government funding
5. Individual gifts
6. Major gifts
7. Special events

Projected expenses should include:
1. Consultants (as needed for planning, training, coaching, strategies, and marketing)
2. Contingency fees
3. Direct mail, including list rental fees, printing, and postage
4. Donor management software, including training, lease fees, upgrades, and technical support

5. Donor recognition, including certificates, plaques, and other gifts of thanks for donors, volunteers, and visitors
6. Event costs — small receptions, breakfasts/lunches, or a large gala, depending upon your plan
7. Graphic design and printing
8. Marketing materials, such as brochures, audiovisual products, annual reports, case statements, ad slicks, and invitations (design and printing)
9. Photography
10. Postage
11. Research
12. Staff development
13. Staff salary and benefits (including the percentage of time spent by non-fundraising staff on fundraising activities)
14. Travel
15. Website design

## Funds And Resources Checklist

Use the following checklist as you review the allocation of your funds and resources.

| APPLIES TO YOUR ORGANIZATION | DESCRIPTION |
|---|---|
| ☐ Yes ☐ No ☐ Not Sure | We have identified the costs that we will incur as we implement our fundraising plan. |
| | Comments: |
| ☐ Yes ☐ No ☐ Not Sure | We have identified our potential sources of revenue and defined a financial goal for each source. |
| | Comments: |
| ☐ Yes ☐ No ☐ Not Sure | We have created a budget that reflects projected revenue and fundraising-related expenses. |
| | Comments: |

| APPLIES TO YOUR ORGANIZATION | DESCRIPTION |
|---|---|
| ☐ Yes ☐ No ☐ Not Sure | We monitor our budget on a monthly basis and make adjustments each quarter. |
| | Comments: |
| ☐ Yes ☐ No ☐ Not Sure | We have identified costs that can be offset by in-kind gifts of products and services. |
| | Comments: |
| ☐ Yes ☐ No ☐ Not Sure | We have calculated the cost per dollar raised as a percentage of our fundraising goal. |
| | Comments: |
| ☐ Yes ☐ No ☐ Not Sure | Our fundraising leadership team understands the concept of the cost per dollar raised and is able to talk about this with potential donors. |
| | Comments: |
| ☐ Yes ☐ No ☐ Not Sure | Our chief financial officer has reviewed and approved our fundraising budget. |
| | Comments: |
| ☐ Yes ☐ No ☐ Not Sure | Our chief financial officer ensures that fundraising expenses and revenue are accurately tracked. |
| | Comments: |

## What Next?

If you have achieved all or most of the items on the above checklist, well done! Financial planning and monitoring are vital yet challenging components of any fundraising effort. Over time, as budgets grow and revenue sources evolve, revisit this list as a reminder of the basic steps needed to maintain financial solvency and strong fiscal literacy and transparency within your organization.

If you answered no to some of the questions, or aren't certain of the answers, *now* is the time to address these challenges. Fundraising should not proceed without an accurate accounting of the costs, revenues, budgets, and goals associated with your plan. If your staff or leadership lack the technical skills to tackle these topics, consider seeking outside counsel. (Check local libraries or community centers for financial literacy workshops. Some accountants, financial planners, and universities offer pro bono services to non-profits.) Invest the time, effort, and resources necessary to establish a sound financial plan for your organization. Without this foundation, the effectiveness of your future fundraising dollars could be compromised.

**Notes:**_____

_____

_____


**Three Actions I Will Take:**

1. _____

2. _____

3. _____

CHAPTER 5

# Telling Your Story

*Create a clear, concise, and compelling case for financial support that ties back to the organization's strategic plan.*

The **case for support** is at the heart of all fundraising. It needs to be clear, concise, and compelling. This document should make the case for why an individual, corporation, foundation, or funding agency should support your fundraising initiative. Fundraising is a competitive endeavor — if you are not raising funds for your organization, someone else is raising money for theirs. It is important that your organization can make the case for why your project is important — what makes it unique. The "case" is used as the basis for verbal and written introductions and solicitations of time, services, goods, and money. It is the basis for all "asks" and should communicate the following:

1. Why: Why should an individual, foundation, corporation, funding agency, or other body choose to invest its time, money, resources, and relationships in this initiative?

2. Need and cost: What will the money be used for? Are you raising funds for a specific program? Advocacy campaign? Building? For a comprehensive fundraising campaign that includes multiple projects? What are the needs associated with each program/project? How much needs to be raised and how will the funds be used?

3.  Projected outcomes: What will happen as a result of a donor's gift? What will be the impact of a gift at a specific level on the organization, constituency, and/or donor? What will happen as a result of the organization's reaching its fundraising goal?
4.  Organization's track record: What are your successes? What have you accomplished?
5.  Organization's history: What caused your organization to come into existence? How have your strategies and approaches changed over time?
6.  Goals: What are the goals identified in your current strategic plan?
7.  Logistics: What will it take for the initiative to be successful — money, time, partnerships? Be specific. Identify what you need.
8.  Benefits: What will donors get in return for their giving that is meaningful to them? This can include community leadership recognition, their name on a building, access to people they want to build a relationship with, or other benefits with real or perceived value in your community.

Fundraising is about asking people to financially support your organization. How will you respond when you are asked what the money will be used for? Can you succinctly communicate the quantitative impact your organization makes, how many people it serves, and how the organization's programs relate to its mission? What if you are asked, "What's in it for me?" The answers to all of these questions — and more! — should be included in your case for support.

Some organizations believe their "cause" is worthy in and of itself. No one questions that money is needed for scholarships, health care, and services that break the cycles of homelessness, poverty, or violence. But how do you answer when someone asks, "What specifically does your organization do with my money?" For example, if funds go to scholarships, do you know how many were awarded last year, the average size, and the selection criteria? Do you know if scholarship recipients remain in contact with your organization, or if you provide support other than scholarships to help ensure students' success?

If your organization provides social services, do you know how many people are served? What types of services they receive and for what period of time? Can you, for example, state what it costs to provide health care access to one individual or one family, or how many families are currently served, and how many could be served with increased funds?

If these sound like questions no one will ask, don't worry — they will be asked. It's just a matter of when. If you are not asked at first, you will be eventually, perhaps at the time and place you most don't want to be put on the spot, so don't be caught unprepared!

Raising money requires a **clear, concise, and compelling** statement that communicates where your organization wants to be in three to five years and what it will cost to get there. It should resonate with your target donors; create excitement and a desire to be affiliated with the organization; and, most importantly, it needs to stimulate giving. Because there are so many worthy causes for people to give their time, money, and resources to, your case for support needs to show how your organization is unique, how the need you address is critical, and how donors' involvement will make a difference.

The case for support is not a literary piece; it is a sales and marketing document that clearly and concisely communicates what you are selling, why someone should give, and what the impact would be. It is rooted in the organization's mission, reflects its values and place in the market, and is based on realistic financial projections.

## Creating Your Case For Support

Imagine yourself in the following scenario: The leadership of a college is in 100 percent agreement regarding the need to renovate its dormitories as a way to better address the expectations of current and prospective residential students. A committee has been formed that has researched the ideal configurations for student living, an architect has created initial drawings, and a contractor has provided you with initial cost estimates. You know the college needs new dorms — the bathroom sinks are old and leaky, the roof needs to be replaced, Wi-Fi is not available, and the windows no longer close all the way. Sometimes it seems as though the list of problems grows on a daily basis. Renovating (or replacing) current student housing is a college priority that is understood by the administration, staff, and students.

**But**, how will you communicate this need to your current and potential donors? Will your message be, "We need to build a new dorm"? Or will you communicate your vision for the growth of your college and how it meets the needs of local residents and those who come from across the state, across the country, and around the world?

In fundraising terms, will you make the case for building new housing or for investing in a new generation of students?

These are the kinds of discussions you need to have as you create the case for support that you will test during the feasibility study.

It is also important to remember that the specific project you are raising money for may not immediately resonate with donors. In the preceding example, the college's leadership wants to raise money to renovate student housing, but that may not be what donors want to fund. The donors may instead prefer to give for new science facilities, and want the college to borrow funds for dorm construction.

Conducting feasibility interviews will provide you with information you need to know before you begin fundraising. This will help you design a fundraising initiative that matches the needs of your institution with donors who want to help you reach those goals. The next chapter discusses the feasibility study process in detail.

## Case For Support Checklist

We suggest that you review the following checklist as you prepare or revise your case for support. We also suggest that you circulate a copy of the checklist with a draft copy of your case for support. Ask board members and staff to review the case for support against the checklist and sign off on it.

**Our organization's case for support is clear, concise, and compelling.  It is no more than three pages long and includes the following:**

| APPLIES TO YOUR ORGANIZATION | DESCRIPTION |
| --- | --- |
| ☐ Yes <br> ☐ No <br> ☐ Not Sure | An organizational history that includes significant dates, accomplishments, and/or milestones. <br> A description of where we are today, including: <br> a.  Who we serve/advocate for <br> b.  How we serve them/advocate for them <br> c.  How we are unique — what we do best <br> d.  How our work serves a critical need |
| | Comments: |

| APPLIES TO YOUR ORGANIZATION | DESCRIPTION |
|---|---|
| ☐ Yes<br>☐ No<br>☐ Not Sure | Current quantifiable outcomes and successes — the number of people served or advocated for, the number of policy advances secured, awards or public recognition received, etc.<br>Comments: |
| ☐ Yes<br>☐ No<br>☐ Not Sure | Projected (future) quantifiable outcomes.<br>Comments: |
| ☐ Yes<br>☐ No<br>☐ Not Sure | Our mission statement.<br>*Our mission statement ties back to our strategic plan.*<br>Comments: |
| ☐ Yes<br>☐ No<br>☐ Not Sure | How we are qualified to deliver on our mission.<br>Comments: |
| ☐ Yes<br>☐ No<br>☐ Not Sure | Our vision for where we want to be in three to five years.<br>Comments: |
| ☐ Yes<br>☐ No<br>☐ Not Sure | How we plan to implement our vision.<br>*Our vision ties back to our strategic plan.*<br>Comments: |
| ☐ Yes<br>☐ No<br>☐ Not Sure | What it will cost to implement our vision.<br>Comments: |
| ☐ Yes<br>☐ No<br>☐ Not Sure | An overview of what we are raising money for.<br>Comments: |

| APPLIES TO YOUR ORGANIZATION | DESCRIPTION |
|---|---|
| ☐ Yes<br>☐ No<br>☐ Not Sure | Why these funds are needed.<br><br>Comments: |
| ☐ Yes<br>☐ No<br>☐ Not Sure | Costs associated with tangible program outcomes, not organizational expenses.<br>*For example:* "$100,000 to increase the number of youth served from 350 to 500," instead of "$100,000 to hire two new case workers."<br><br>Comments: |
| ☐ Yes<br>☐ No<br>☐ Not Sure | Why an individual, business, corporation, or charitable foundation should give to our organization.<br>*For example:*<br>• "Support of our organization helps increase the number of individuals with job training that meets local workforce needs."<br>• "Your gift helps ensure access to health care for those most in need."<br><br>Comments: |
| ☐ Yes<br>☐ No<br>☐ Not Sure | The quantifiable impact that gifts at specific levels will make.<br>*For example:*<br>• "A gift of $1,500 will provide one student with books for one semester."<br>• "$35 provides one low-income working mother with money for gas to get to work for a week."<br>• "Every $1 you give helps provide five meals for residents in need."<br><br>Comments: |

| APPLIES TO YOUR ORGANIZATION | DESCRIPTION |
|---|---|
| ☐ Yes ☐ No ☐ Not Sure | The tangible and intangible benefits a donor or sponsor will receive. |
| | Comments: |
| ☐ Yes ☐ No ☐ Not Sure | How donors and sponsors will be recognized for their giving. |
| | Comments: |
| ☐ Yes ☐ No ☐ Not Sure | Excitement, a sense of vitality. *People reading this document want to financially give to our organization, be affiliated with us, and get involved.* |
| | Comments: |
| ☐ Yes ☐ No ☐ Not Sure | Quotes from key stakeholders and influencers such as major funders and donors, community/political leaders, or those served by or positively impacted by our work. |
| | Comments: |
| ☐ Yes ☐ No ☐ Not Sure | List of board members, with their affiliations. |
| | Comments: |
| ☐ Yes ☐ No ☐ Not Sure | List of key staff members, with their credentials/qualifications. |
| | Comments: |
| ☐ Yes ☐ No ☐ Not Sure | List of advisory council members. |
| | Comments: |

# Reminder

For optimal effectiveness, a case for support must have the full support of board members and staff. All team members should be fluent and vested in the contents of the case. This can be achieved by involving each of them in its development and/or revision. Along with asking them to consult the above checklist, solicit input through open-ended questions such as "What is the greatest strength and the primary weakness of this document?" or "How would you improve this case for support?" If contrasting opinions emerge, seek out the root of those differences and strive to build consensus. All input should be valued and given serious consideration. This internal review process is time well spent — the feedback you receive will bolster your case for support and prepare it for public vetting during the feasibility study process and beyond.

**Notes:**_____

_____

_____

**Three Actions I Will Take:**

1. _____

2. _____

3. _____

CHAPTER 6

# Assessing the Need

*Complete a fundraising assessment and feasibility study or survey.*

Private sector businesses engage in market research before they launch a new product or attempt to secure capital investment. Non-profit institutions need to do the same. This market research is referred to as a fundraising assessment and feasibility study (or survey). Such a study or survey will provide your institution with the necessary pre-fundraising "market research" and is used to:

1.  Assess the institution's position and standing in the marketplace
2.  Identify prospective donors, volunteer leadership, and new constituencies
3.  Assess whether or not it will be feasible for the initiative to meet its financial goal within the projected time frame
4.  Identify initial levels of financial and in-kind support available
5.  Help secure buy-in from key stakeholders
6.  Create early awareness of intent to launch a fundraising initiative
7.  Assess level of internal fundraising capacity and infrastructure

The study should be conducted by a fund development or fundraising firm so that those interviewed have a higher sense of confidentiality, and so that existing relationships are not strained by the questions asked or the answers given. It is crucial that those interviewed provide honest responses. Many times what is said in an interview conducted by a fund development firm is different from what a current or prospective donor or funder would say when questioned directly by a board member or senior staff.

## How Do You Know What You Don't Know?

Working together, your board, executive director, and development director can determine the amount of funds to be raised annually or for a specific project. They can define how the funds will be used and why they are needed. But, will people outside your organization or institution agree with their assessment? Will they understand why the money is needed and how, for example, paying salaries, rent, and insurance translate into reduced poverty for local residents? Will they actually give to your organization and encourage others to do so? You can sit in a room for days trying to answer these questions. Or you can conduct a feasibility study.

A feasibility study is the process of interviewing individuals who can provide funding, resources, and influence that will facilitate the success of your proposed fundraising. It also includes interviews with those you believe may oppose your organization and its quest to raise money. The purpose of these interviews is to uncover how your community responds to your proposed fundraising before you begin the process of asking people for money.

Whether a study or a survey, the process should include 12 to 45 (or more) interviews that are conducted in person, when possible. The number of interviews is influenced by the amount of money you seek to raise. A study provides key findings, suggested next steps, and detailed analysis of the responses to each question, including statistics for how each question was answered and an analysis of the responses to each question. A survey typically includes key findings and suggested next steps. The main difference between the two is cost and time — a study takes more time and costs more money. (It is also required of institutions preparing to raise large sums of money, as the detailed analysis provides a higher level of due diligence.)

In both cases, the information obtained from the interviewees is not attributed to specific individuals. This allows those interviewed to speak freely without having to consider, "What will they think of me if they know this is how I really feel?" There are many reasons people have for not sharing important information directly with the leadership of an organization. Many will, however, share their true thoughts when interviewed, knowing that the information is kept confidential and is needed so the organization can improve its operations and fundraising.

Conducting a feasibility study or survey requires a case for support document for interviewees to read before their interview. This document outlines your organization's mission, vision, successes, leadership, how much you want to raise, how the funds will be used, and the impact this will make.

There are several reasons the study or survey should be conducted by a consultant:
1.  People will often tell a consultant things they are unwilling to say to the executive director or an individual associated with your organization.
2.  It is rare for an organization to have staff or board members who know how to conduct a feasibility study or survey and analyze the results.

## What You Can Learn By Conducting A Fundraising Feasibility Study

Too often organizations are focused on how quickly they can begin fundraising. "We need the money now!" is a common cry. Our response is simply, "It's not how quickly you begin raising money, it's how quickly you reach your fundraising goal."

You can begin raising money without finding out how local stakeholders and potential donors respond to the specifics of your campaign, but the real question is, will you raise the money you need. Fundraising campaigns that launch without the market research that a fundraising feasibility study provides can later find themselves in the midst of what is known as campaign stall — they have raised a percentage of their goal, but they can't raise the remaining funds.

Conducting a fundraising feasibility study or survey is one way to avoid such stall. This is because the results of the study will let you know important information such as:
1.  How do those interviewed really feel about your proposed fundraising campaign? Do they understand what you are raising money for and how those funds will help you deliver on your mission?
2.  Do your current and prospective donors believe the organization or institution is headed in the right direction?
3.  How do they rate your CEO, board members, and staff?

4. Do people believe your organization fulfills an important role in the community? Do they know your mission, vision, and major programs?
5. Are they willing to give to your proposed fundraising campaign? Why or why not? If yes, at what level? If no, would they consider making a gift at a later date?
6. Are there others they know of who they believe would want to financially support your organization?
7. Who can provide volunteer fundraising leadership? Who amongst those interviewed would be willing to give of their time to help you raise the money you need? Who else do they recommend to provide such leadership?
8. Who can provide in-kind resources to help offset costs associated with fundraising and annual operations? Can a local company provide your printing? Can a realtor help you secure donated office space?
9. Most importantly, do those interviewed believe you can reach your fundraising goal, and how much time do they believe it will take for you to do so?

Pay close attention to the last point. If the people you intend to ask to financially support your organization are not willing to do so, it is crucial that you understand their objections, take the time to address them (if appropriate), and find other individuals and institutions that feel more favorably toward your organization and its leadership, mission, and goals.

The information gained from feasibility interviews can help you modify your proposed fundraising strategies and activities. It can also help you address the concerns of those interviewed and take advantage of opportunities you may not have otherwise known of.

## Getting Ready For A Feasibility Study

Contracting with a fund development firm for a fundraising assessment and feasibility study is a milestone investment. It means your institution is ready and willing to learn what it will take for the proposed fundraising initiative or campaign to be successful.

It also means a lot of work. Before you can hire a firm to conduct a study you will need to have accomplished the following:
1. Identified what you are raising money for and how much you need to raise over what period of time

2. Allocated resources to pay for the fundraising assessment and feasibility study
3. Created a well-defined draft case for support or fundraising brochure to test during the interviews

The work of preparing for an assessment and feasibility study often takes more time and energy than originally imagined.

## Reviewing The Results And Next Steps

The results of a study should be reviewed with an open mind. Because these studies often reveal hidden assets and challenges, there can be a tendency to "hide" the results from the institution's full leadership. We recommend against this. If the report reveals challenges or weaknesses, chances are great that many people already know about these, whether or not they choose to publicly acknowledge this. Sharing unexpected information — and taking action to address problems that surfaced — is risky, but it also helps build a culture of transparency and accountability.

A well-produced study will include suggested next steps. Review these carefully and implement those that you can. This will help you take advantage of opportunities and address challenges uncovered through the fundraising assessment and feasibility study process.

## Who Should Be Interviewed

Identifying new potential donors and volunteer leadership is a primary reason for conducting feasibility interviews. Another reason is to ensure that the opinions and perspectives of current major donors and stakeholders are incorporated into your planning.

Ideally, the fundraising assessment and feasibility study should include interviews with those individuals who can impact your fundraising in a positive way, as well as those who could present challenges. The following is a list of the types of individuals to consider. The people you select should reflect your organization's position, mission, and fundraising goals.

1. Board chair
2. Board members
3. Business leaders (local, regional, and national)
4. Chair of the board's development committee

5. Chief executive officer, president, or executive director
6. Current and lapsed major donors
7. Elected and appointed government officials
8. Individuals opposed to or critical of your institution and/or its leadership.
9. Individuals who can positively influence the outcome of the proposed fundraising activities
10. Individuals you serve or have served in the past
11. Leaders of competitive and complementary institutions
12. Long-term annual donors
13. Philanthropists who give to similar institutions
14. Relevant foundation executives or program officers
15. Religious and lay leaders or members of local faith organizations
16. Staff members, including those responsible for fundraising, public relations, or communications, and those who lead the specific programs your institution is known for
17. Alumni (if applicable)

## Potential Interviewee Checklist

Before you work with the potential interviewee checklist, take a moment to do the following:

1. Identify the individuals who currently provide leadership, financial support, and guidance to your institution.
2. **Identify the individuals who can influence the success of your fundraising. Be sure to include those you know, as well as those you don't yet have a relationship with.**
3. Determine the number of interviews you need to conduct in order to provide a diverse sampling of opinions and information.
4. Multiply the number of interviewees you need to conduct by three. (This is important because it can be challenging to secure interviews. Having a pool of potential interviewees that is three times the number of people you want to interview will help ensure that you secure the targeted number of interviews.)

After you have addressed these four questions, you are ready to create your list of potential interviewees using the following checklist. As you enter the potential interviewees' information, remember to indicate the reason why you are including each person, along with his or her priority rating. For example, should an individual be in the first round of people asked to participate or should she be asked as a second choice if others are unavailable?

# Sample checklist:

| Name | Affiliation | Reason to Interview | Rating |
|---|---|---|---|
| Dr. Janice Williams | Provost, George Washington University | Former faculty member; has given $150/year for seven of the past ten years | #1 |
| Mr. Winston Long | Founder, Everyday Systems | Former patient; received life-saving medical care | #1 |
| Annie Johnson | Senior Vice President, Farmers Bank | Local business leader, influencer, and donor | #1 |
| Pastor Clifford Raymond | New Haven Baptist Church | Respected religious leader | #2 |
| Jeannie Akbari | Chair, National Health Council | Board member | #1 |
| Michael Garzouzi | CEO, Killer Baking Company | City council member | #2 |
| Willie Marshall Parks | Retired, County Administrator | Long-term donor and volunteer | #2 |

Use the following checklist as you create your list of priority interviewees.

| Name | Affiliation | Reason to Interview | Rating |
|---|---|---|---|
|  |  |  |  |
|  |  |  |  |
|  |  |  |  |
|  |  |  |  |
|  |  |  |  |
|  |  |  |  |
|  |  |  |  |
|  |  |  |  |
|  |  |  |  |
|  |  |  |  |
|  |  |  |  |
|  |  |  |  |

# What Next?

Once you've identified and prioritized a list of potential interviewees, it's time to ask for their participation. Even if you have contracted with a fund development firm or other third-party organization to conduct the interviews, you will need to make the initial contact and secure the interview. The appropriate form for this communication depends on the person and his or her connection to the organization. If a board member has a close relationship with a potential interviewee, task her with letting a potential interviewee know he will be contacted about participating in a feasibility interview.

All potential interviewees should be contacted by the board president or executive director via by letter. The note should explain briefly that your organization would be honored if they would participate in a feasibility study being conducted on your behalf. Follow up by phone call if necessary. If an individual agrees to be interviewed, secure a date, time and location for the interview. Avoid discussing details about your organization or the study; state only that you are seeking honest and anonymous feedback about the organization's fundraising plan, and that you've secured an outside party to conduct a survey. Thank her in advance for her participation. The names and contact information of all willing participants should be submitted to your fund development firm.

Struggling to come up with enough names for a meaningful feasibility study? Try a "snowball" approach: among the core group of interviewees you've identified, ask each to suggest at least three other people whom they believe could provide helpful input. Ideally, this request should be made at the conclusion of each participant's interview, after she or he has reviewed your case for support and is best poised to recommend other relevant interviewees.

---

**Three Actions I Will Take:**

1. _____

2. _____

3. _____

---

CHAPTER 7

# Building Your Road Map

*Develop a time-phased fundraising plan.*

Creating and working from a fundraising plan is an important prerequisite for fundraising success. Whether you serve as an executive director, board member, fundraising staff, or volunteer, there is a role for you to play. It takes a well-orchestrated team to ensure an organization's financial goals are met, and working from a plan helps increase the odds you will be successful.

## Getting Started

The amount of money you will need to raise should be derived from your annual organizational budget or special campaign budget. This budget should be developed as a team effort with information solicited from both staff and board leadership. It should reflect realistic revenue and cost projections and include funds for the work of fundraising. Once the budget is approved by the board, it is the responsibility of the board and staff to ensure that revenue projections are met. Most organizations and institutions have several different revenue sources. These can include fees, tuition, and other forms of earned revenue; government grants; grants from local foundations; revenue from special events; gifts from individuals, families, organizations, businesses, and others; and bequests and planned gifts.

While different individuals or departments within an organization or institution may be responsible for revenue from specific sources, we suggest you create a development team that includes a representative from each revenue-producing department, program, or division. This helps ensure that all parties are aware of the progress being made in meeting revenue projections and helps create a culture that values transparency and accountability.

The ability of staff, board members, and volunteers to raise money is contingent upon the organization's fundraising **capacity**. This can be assessed formally by outside fundraising counsel or informally by staff. Items that affect capacity include the number of staff, board members, and volunteers, and the extent of their fundraising experience; management information and reporting systems; commitment of the executive director and board; adequacy of the fundraising budget; marketing/communications plan; and number and quality of current relationships with donors and prospective funders.

Once you know your capacity and how much money you need to raise, you can begin to create your **fundraising plan**.

Keep in mind that no two fundraising plans are alike. Your fundraising plan should be an easy-to-use document that clearly communicates to all parties what you are seeking to achieve and how you intend to reach these goals. It should be referred to on a regular basis; the printed versions should become tattered from use. Your plan should:

1. Tie to the programmatic and financial goals identified in your strategic plan
2. Be designed to engage the specific constituency (or constituencies) identified through the fundraising assessment and feasibility study
3. Serve as the blueprint or road map for your fundraising activities
4. Include a timeline that identifies activities and milestones on a quarter-by-quarter basis, along with the individuals responsible for ensuring each activity is completed and each milestone is met
5. Include roles and responsibilities for volunteers, board members, staff, and consultants
6. Identify revenue sources and a financial goal for each source
7. Outline strategies for securing funds from each source
8. Include an organization chart that illustrates how board members, volunteers, and staff will work with other
9. Include a gift chart showing how many gifts at specific levels will need to be secured

# Preparing Your Plan

Here are a few action items to focus on as you create your plan.

## Determine your fundraising goal and related expenses.

Your plan should clearly communicate how much money you are seeking to raise and the sources it could come from. It should also include a draft or projected fundraising budget. The budget should identify potential revenue sources and a financial goal for each source. It should also identify projected expenses related to implementing the plan. (Refer to chapter 4, beginning on page 19, for more detailed information on creating your fundraising budget.)

## Develop your timeline and activity chart.

Your fundraising plan should include a detailed timeline and activity chart. This chart should serve as a project management tool to help ensure that activities are completed on time, fundraising activities stay on schedule, and due dates for dependent activities are not delayed.

For example, if one of your major fundraising activities is an annual gala, you know from experience that many tasks are dependent upon the successful completion of earlier tasks. For the event to meet its revenue projections, invited guests need to have information about the specifics of the event at least several months in advance. That means the talent may need to be booked four to six months in advance. Depending upon where you are located, you may need to secure your ideal location a year in advance. Sponsors also need to be secured. Save-the-date cards and printed invitations need to be designed and produced. Billboards need to go up. Public service announcements need to be produced and distributed. Delays in accomplishing any of these activities hamper the ability of volunteers and staff to meet their deadlines for subsequent activities.

Care, attention, and planning are required. Close attention to detail and frequent communication amongst all parties will help keep your timeline and activity chart up to date and will support your fundraising.

If you have time, talk with a construction manager or software developer about the importance of project management. You will quickly see how some of the "inevitable" challenges that arise within fundraising can be minimized through the use of project management principles and techniques, including the utilization of what we refer to as a timeline and activity chart.

Here is a simple example of what we mean:

| ACTIVITY | PERSON RESPONSIBLE | Q1 | Q2 | Q3 | Q4 |
|---|---|---|---|---|---|
| Solicit donors who have given $1,000+ per year for four years for a multi-year pledge or increased annual gift | Major gifts volunteers | | | | x |

You may wish to include more detail (see example below) for improved communication.

| ACTIVITY | PERSON RESPONSIBLE | Q1 | Q2 | Q3 | Q4 |
|---|---|---|---|---|---|
| Identify donors who have given gifts of $1,000 or more for four years or more | Data specialist | x | | | |
| Review list with fundraising team | Development director | x | | | |
| Determine an increased ask amount for each donor for upcoming appeal | Development team | x | | | |
| Assign each donor to a volunteer who will call or visit with the donor | Development director | | x | | |
| Provide volunteers with contact information for each assigned donor and updated information about the organization's impact | Development director | | x | | |
| Host solicitation training and role-playing sessions for volunteers | | | | | |
| Solicit donors who have given $1,000 or more a year for four years for a multi-year pledge or increased annual gift | Major gift volunteers | | x | x | x |

| ACTIVITY | PERSON RESPONSIBLE | Q1 | Q2 | Q3 | Q4 |
|---|---|---|---|---|---|
| Write up results from each phone call and submit to development director | Major gift volunteers | | x | x | x |
| Make personal phone calls to thank donors for their gifts | Major gift volunteers; executive director | | x | x | x |

When you create your timeline and activity chart,

1. Identify the important tasks to be completed throughout the life of the fundraising initiative, with due dates for each. Enter these on your quarterly or monthly timeline and activity chart.
2. After this first pass, think about what other activities will need to be completed in order for the initial list of activities to be successful. Enter these on your quarterly or monthly timeline and activity chart.
3. Identify who is responsible for ensuring that each activity is completed on time.

Be sure you have someone assigned to maintaining (and updating) the chart and circulating updated versions to everyone who needs the information. Use the chart during your development team meetings to report on progress and make modifications as circumstances require.

## Define roles and responsibilities.

Roles and responsibilities should be created for volunteers, board members, staff, and consultants. There is no shortcut here. If people don't know what is expected of them, it is hard for them to meet expectations. And it is very difficult to evaluate staff or volunteers when you haven't clearly identified what is expected of them. Take the time to document roles and responsibilities before you engage volunteers and hire staff.

When you have defined what you want people to do, it is easier for you to determine if you are asking the right people to volunteer for key fundraising positions. Likewise, it is easier to evaluate potential staff members when you know the skill set required and what you expect each staff person to be responsible for. (For a more detailed discussion about roles and responsibilities, see chapter 8, beginning on page 51.)

## Create your gift chart.

Fundraising is both an art and a science. One of the fundraising "sciences" is the creation of the prospect/gift chart. Creating this chart helps ensure your organization cultivates and solicits enough people to meet your financial goal. The "gift chart" helps determine how many prospective donors need to be identified for each gift you want to receive. It reduces guesswork and impresses upon all parties the amount of work required for success.

While it takes work to create and use a gift chart, we recommend this method over the "we could get a big gift from Bill Gates, Bill Cosby, Oprah Winfrey ..." tactic. **It is sobering to realize that raising $300,000 could require you to identify as many as 2,691 prospective donors.** That is a much larger number of prospects than most organizations or institutions are prepared to work with. It illustrates why fundraising must be an integral and ongoing responsibility shared by all staff, board members, and volunteers.

Below is a sample gift chart for an organization seeking to raise $300,000 for annual operations, followed by information on how to interpret it.

| | | | | | | | |
|---|---|---|---|---|---|---|---|
| **SAMPLE GIFT CHART** | | | | | | | |
| **$300,000 FUNDRAISING GOAL** | | | | | | | |
| Gift Range | Number of Prospects | Cumulative Number of Prospects | Number of Gifts | Cumulative Number of Gifts | Prospect/Gift Ratio | Dollar per Range | Cumulative Total |
| $30,000 | 5 | 5 | 1 | 1 | 5:1 | $30,000 | $30,000 |
| $15,000 | 10 | 15 | 2 | 3 | 5:1 | $30,000 | $60,000 |
| $7,500 | 20 | 35 | 4 | 7 | 5:1 | $30,000 | $90,000 |
| $4,000 | 40 | 75 | 8 | 15 | 5:1 | $32,000 | $122,000 |
| $2,000 | 64 | 139 | 16 | 31 | 4:1 | $32,000 | $154,000 |
| $1,000 | 128 | 267 | 32 | 63 | 4:1 | $32,000 | $186,000 |
| $500 | 192 | 459 | 64 | 127 | 3:1 | $32,000 | $218,000 |
| $250 | 384 | 843 | 128 | 255 | 3:1 | $32,000 | $250,000 |
| **First tier of donors** | | | **31% of gifts and 83% of goal** | | | | |
| $125 | 768 | 1,611 | 256 | 511 | 3:1 | $32,000 | $282,000 |
| $50 | 1,080 | 2,691 | 360 | 871 | 3:1 | $18,000 | $300,000 |
| **Second tier of donors** | | | **69% of gifts and 17% of goal** | | | | |

Raising $300,000 will require a lead gift of $30,000 (10 percent of the goal). Securing that gift will require five "qualified prospective donors." A qualified prospective donor is a person or an organization with a demonstrated interest in your organization and the financial means to make the gift you are soliciting.

You will also need to secure two gifts of $15,000, four gifts of $7,500, and eight gifts of $4,000. The sample gift chart illustrates the following fundraising principles:

- The lead gift is 10 percent of the fundraising goal. There should be five prospects identified for the lead gift.
- The next gift represents half of the lead gift. (Use a 5:1 ratio of prospects to gifts.)
- The next gift represents half of the previous gift. (Use a 5:1 ratio of prospects to gifts.)

These numbers and ratios are suggested for annual fundraising. They are a basic starting point and should be adjusted up or down depending upon your institution's fundraising experience. If your institution is new to fundraising, we suggest a higher prospect-to-gift ratio as a way to help you reach your financial goal. With more experience and stronger relationships with your donors you can consider lowering the ratios.

Keep the following fundraising principles in mind when creating your gift chart:

1. The majority of time should be allocated to identifying, cultivating, soliciting, and retaining your largest donors. Prospective donors need to be constantly identified, cultivated, and solicited throughout the year.
2. The majority of funds will come from your largest donors (an estimated 80 percent of funds from about 20 percent of donors).
3. The number of gifts to be solicited is often greater than expected.
4. **Every solicitation does not result in gift.**
5. Fundraising is a numbers game. If one prospective donor declines to give, you need to have another appropriate prospect you can solicit instead.

Taking the time to prepare your prospect/gift chart will help your organization or institution determine how its fundraising leadership and resources should be allocated. The chart should be referred to throughout the year to measure your progress.

## Add more detail.

After you develop your gift chart, you can add another level of detail: include the names of qualified prospective donors. This will make clear whether or not your organization has identified enough prospective donors to reach its goal. If you don't have enough — or some decline to give — you know you need to increase your cultivation activities or make adjustments to your fundraising goal.

# Fundraising Plan Checklist

Use the following checklist as you create your fundraising plan.

| | Our Fund Development Plan... |
|---|---|
| ☐ Yes <br> ☐ No <br> ☐ Not Sure | Is based on information from our fundraising assessment and feasibility study or survey. <br><br> Comments: |
| ☐ Yes <br> ☐ No <br> ☐ Not Sure | Includes input from the executive director, board chair, chief fundraising officer, chief financial officer, current and long-term donors, and volunteers. <br><br> Comments: |
| ☐ Yes <br> ☐ No <br> ☐ Not Sure | Is easy to read and understand. <br><br> Comments: |
| ☐ Yes <br> ☐ No <br> ☐ Not Sure | Includes a projected budget with fundraising-related expenses and projected revenue (with sources). <br><br> Comments: |
| ☐ Yes <br> ☐ No <br> ☐ Not Sure | Includes roles and responsibilities for volunteers, board members, staff, and consultants. <br><br> Comments: |
| ☐ Yes <br> ☐ No <br> ☐ Not Sure | Includes an organization chart. <br><br> Comments: |
| ☐ Yes <br> ☐ No <br> ☐ Not Sure | Includes a gift chart. <br><br> Comments: |
| ☐ Yes <br> ☐ No <br> ☐ Not Sure | Includes a timeline and an activity chart. <br><br> Comments: |

| | OUR FUND DEVELOPMENT PLAN... |
|---|---|
| ☐ Yes ☐ No ☐ Not Sure | Identifies revenue sources and a financial goal for each source. |
| | Comments: |
| ☐ Yes ☐ No ☐ Not Sure | Has been reviewed and accepted by the executive director/CEO and development director, and approved by the board of directors. |
| | Comments: |

The eventual success of your fundraising efforts are dependent upon the time and resources you invest in developing a solid fundraising plan. The tasks outlined in this chapter are meant to be challenging; a feasible fundraising plan requires hard work from executive leadership, board members, and staff. Do not become discouraged or tempted to take shortcuts. Remember, you are creating a road map to success. Your fundraising plan should be thorough, well researched, and easy to follow. Most importantly, it should provide a solid foundation for your future fundraising activities.

**Notes:**_____

_____

_____

**Three Actions I Will Take:**

1. _____

2. _____

3. _____

CHAPTER 8

# Division of Labor

***Define roles and responsibilities for staff, board members, volunteers, and consultants.***

Defined roles and responsibilities for staff, consultants, board members, and volunteers help ensure that your fundraising activities run smoothly. When team members know their roles and responsibilities, they are more inclined to take action. No one person is being asked to do it all; each has a specific role to play. Roles and responsibilities should be documented and presented to prospective volunteers when they are invited to join the fundraising initiative.

This takes time. Ideally, roles and responsibilities should be documented in your fundraising plan. If you haven't already done so, stop and take a moment for this work. It is important and greatly increases volunteer (and staff!) retention and productivity. It is much easier for people to meet the mark when they know what it is.

1.  Here are some things to think about as you create fundraising-related roles and responsibilities.
2.  What are the skills, experiences, connections, and personal attributes that a volunteer, committee member, or staff person needs to possess?
3.  What is this person or committee expected to accomplish or produce?
4.  If there is a fundraising goal that you expect an individual to meet, what is the amount of that financial goal?

5.  If it is a marketing or communications goal that supports fundraising, have you made it clear that marketing and communications activities need to positively impact fundraising? For example, does your communication team understand the importance of placing op-ed pieces, purchasing ad space, or sending out an e-newsletter shortly before you begin to solicit year-end donations? Are members willing to work closely with the fund development team to create awareness and excitement for upcoming fundraising events? Are they prepared to communicate the impact your institution is able to make this year as a result of meeting a specific fundraising goal?

6.  If you are asking an individual or committee to take responsibility for a project such as "fundraising from local faith organizations," be sure to break the project into multiple tasks that can be tracked over time. These tasks are at the heart of roles and responsibilities. Do not be afraid to be specific.

7.  What are the time frames associated with each expectation?

8.  Is this person or committee expected to attend meetings? If so, which meetings and how often?

9.  Which staff members, volunteers, or committees are expected to collaborate, and for what purpose?

10. Who does this person or committee report to? (Who do they turn to for guidance, suggestions, and resources?)

11. Are there reporting requirements? If so, are these verbal, written, or electronic? What is the frequency? Who is the report given to?

12. When preparing roles and responsibilities for current staff or board members, refer to their job descriptions and incorporate essential duties from these descriptions. Expand on them as necessary.

Use your answers to these questions to create a one-paragraph description of the purpose of the position or committee, its financial (and non-financial) goals, and a list of specific tasks. Be specific.

Here a few examples to consider including in a description:

1.  Identify 35 prospective donors who have the interest and financial capacity to make an annual gift of $15,000 each.

2.  Host quarterly "friendraisers" for prospective donors, volunteers, or supporters.

3.  Meet personally with each prospective donor to explore his interests, provide information about our fundraising, and answer questions.

4.  Secure pro-bono printing services for the printing of new brochures.

5. Participate in the process of selecting and testing new donor management software.
6. Provide electronic contact reports after each visit with a current or prospective donor.

If you are writing roles and responsibilities for a committee, be sure to include a list of the types of people who you suggest as potential members. Ideally, the committee chair should invite people she knows to serve with her on the committee. You can always suggest potential members, but remember, it is best to empower your volunteer leadership. Let them attract people they want to work with.

Don't worry that people will reject working with you if you document exactly what it is that you expect them to do. It is much better for people to know your expectations in advance. That way they can give you an honest response as to whether or not they can truly be of service. It also allows volunteers the opportunity to set aside time in advance to fulfill their responsibilities. If someone can't fulfill the roles and responsibilities you have set out, you can mutually negotiate them. Or you can ask someone else to serve instead.

We cannot stress enough how important it is to attract people who are willing and able to fulfill identified roles and responsibilities. It may take you six to nine months to secure a fundraising chair who is willing to solicit lead gifts (10 percent of your fundraising goal) and major gifts. That is much better then quickly attracting a chair who is not willing to solicit gifts at all.

Documented roles and responsibilities should be prepared for:
1. Board chair
2. Board members
3. Fundraising leadership team
4. Executive director
5. Development director
6. Senior staff
7. Fundraising volunteers

# Roles And Responsibilities Checklist

| | DESCRIPTION |
|---|---|
| ☐ Yes<br>☐ No<br>☐ Not Sure | We have identified who we need to write specific roles and responsibilities for. |
| | Comments: |
| ☐ Yes<br>☐ No<br>☐ Not Sure | Roles and responsibilities documents have been prepared for each identified committee, volunteer, or employee. |
| | Comments: |
| ☐ Yes<br>☐ No<br>☐ Not Sure | All volunteers and employees have reviewed their respective roles and responsibilities. |
| | Comments: |
| ☐ Yes<br>☐ No<br>☐ Not Sure | Roles and responsibilities have been revised and updated based on feedback from volunteers and employees. |
| | Comments: |
| ☐ Yes<br>☐ No<br>☐ Not Sure | Orientation or launch meetings have been held for each committee to ensure all members understand their collective and individual roles and responsibilities and have determined how they will organize themselves to meet those goals. |
| | Comments: |

## Tip

Before drafting job descriptions for staff members and volunteers, seek their input. An internal audit of roles and responsibilities provides a helpful starting point for more formal documentation. As appropriate, ask staff, volunteers, and executive leadership to create a comprehensive list of the tasks they complete on a daily, weekly, and monthly basis on behalf of your organization. This accounting will help crystallize the scope of duties required of each position, and may identify gaps or inconsistencies in the workflow. Use this information as you create standardized job descriptions for current and future staff and volunteers.

Notes:_____

_____

_____

**Three Actions I Will Take:**

1. _____

2. _____

3. _____

CHAPTER 9

# Help from Professionals

**Staff**

*Hire professional staff whose primary role is fundraising management, volunteer training and management, and administrative support.*

Fundraising is considered half science, half art. We agree. We also believe that fundraising is a business. To be successful you will need to work with people who know how to conduct the business of fundraising. These can be trained professionals or volunteers who have fundraising experience and expertise. Fundraising is very competitive and can be unforgiving toward those who don't follow fundraising best practices. Take the time to determine the level of professionalism your organization will require to meet its fundraising goals. Make the investment in staff as if your fundraising depends on it, because it does.

Fundraising professionals help ensure that fundraising ethics and standards are communicated, integrated into the organization's management, and adhered to. Volunteers and donors quickly recognize when professionals are guiding your organization's fundraising. This helps build confidence and increase engagement. Donors and volunteers want to know that their gifts of time and money are well managed. Fundraising initiatives tend to stall and/or show little growth when there is a lack of professionalism within the organization's fundraising staff. We believe that fundraising should be volunteer-driven and guided and supported by professional staff.

Take your time and find the right people to meet the criterion and culture of your organization. Don't compromise your organization because of a sense of urgency, lack of current funds, or the desire for a quick fix.

**Create a job description.** Define how you will evaluate your staff, and share the criteria with current and prospective employees. Help ensure your staff are successful by communicating how you want them to allocate their time and what you expect for them to accomplish. Fundraising success is measured by more than "dollars-in-the-door." The money that comes to you today may be the result of relationships built years ago by staff, board members, former clients, volunteers, or others. Current staff need to meet quantifiable goals, such as number of new prospective donors identified, number of personal meetings coordinated by staff, number of solicitations made, number of calls and meetings with volunteers and board members, number of volunteers engaged, and number of prospective donors solicited by volunteers.

**Your most qualified staff will be those who focus on recruiting, engaging, and managing volunteers.** Your volunteers are the people who are often the most passionate about your cause. Volunteers are the people who can talk to potential donors and share with them their experiences. They are the ones who can say, "I believe in this organization, and I make it a priority to give my time and money here."

Volunteers are key to the success of your fundraising. Trained and qualified staff are needed to facilitate the work of volunteers.

Your fundraising will need the support of an individual with strong administrative skills. Big-picture thinkers are wonderful. They are creative. They see the solution when everyone else sees problems. However, these individuals need to be teamed with detailed project managers who follow up on the big ideas and make sure that all steps required for implementation are in motion. **Your success is in the details.** These cannot be overlooked.

It is also important to remember that a person with experience managing special events does not necessarily have the skills required for work with major donors. Similarly, someone experienced as a development director does not necessarily have the skills required for work as a data management specialist.

The following list outlines two types of positions that you may find yourself hiring for.

Your administrative support person can be charged with activities such as:
1.  Updating and maintaining your activity chart
2.  Drafting correspondence on behalf of board members and other volunteers
3.  Updating the donor/prospect/volunteer database
4.  Drafting thank-you letters and gift receipts
5.  Taking minutes at fundraising-related meetings and distributing these within 24 hours

Professional fundraising staff manage and implement your fundraising plan. Their responsibilities include:
1.  Training, orientation, and education in the areas of fundraising, cultivation, solicitation, and stewardship
2.  Coordinating the activities of volunteers, staff, board members, and consultants
3.  Coordinating special events
4.  Designing, implementing, and managing your direct mail program
5.  Managing your Internet fundraising activities
6.  Tracking fundraising activities (project management)
7.  Ensuring all donors and prospects are thanked and acknowledged for their time, gifts, and involvement
8.  Moving the plan forward and ensuring progress toward fundraising goals
9.  Reporting to the board on fundraising progress (funds raised versus fundraising goals)
10. Working with the fundraising leadership team to create strategies needed to meet goals
11. Supporting executive leadership, board members, and leadership-level volunteers through the donor identification, cultivation, solicitation, and stewardship process
12. Soliciting major gifts as appropriate

## Qualities To Look For In A Fundraising Professional

1.  **Strong people skills:** ability to interact well with people from different backgrounds, to make them feel comfortable, and to present information and make an honest human connection with donors, prospects, volunteers, and foundation staff.
2.  **Strong writing skills:** ability to write letters, reports, and short proposals to individual donors, foundation staff, volunteers, and board members. Strong command of the written language.

3.  **Technology skills:** ability to use word processing software, Excel, email, the Internet, and database systems. Working knowledge of databases and how to conduct searches and run reports against the donor database.
4.  Data entry skills: ability to accurately update database information in a timely manner.
5.  **General office skills:** understands the importance of accurate and timely filing of information. Skilled at file maintenance, record keeping, and providing timely responses to donors, volunteers, and staff whether by phone, letter, or email. Courteous and punctual.
6.  **Understanding of development process or sales/marketing cycles:** ability to discern the important and different roles that prospects, volunteers, donors, and staff can play in facilitating giving. Strong general marketing skills and an understanding of the sales and marketing process and cycles.
7.  **Strong time management skills:** ability to work on multiple projects simultaneously, meet (or beat) deadlines, and manage multiple projects and priorities.
8.  **Self-motivated/strong initiative: ability to pursue tasks with a minimum of follow-up or oversight from supervisor.** Willing to ask questions when unsure of next steps.
9.  **Team player:** ability to work well with others and communicate information, successes, and questions.
10. **Strategic thinking:** understands the longer-term implications of short-term goals/tasks and how they relate to increased giving. Ability to grasp the bigger picture as well as the immediate tasks at hand. Strong planning skills.
11. **Strong phone skills:** ability to briefly, warmly, and concisely communicate via phone and voicemail.
12. **Other personal characteristics:** creative, risk-taking, detail-oriented, able to motivate others, and skilled at managing and facilitating activities from a background or behind-the-scenes position.

# Professional Staff Checklist

Use this checklist as you review your organization's utilization of profession staff.

| | DESCRIPTION |
|---|---|
| ☐ Yes<br>☐ No<br>☐ Not Sure | We have assessed the current level of fundraising experience and skills within our staff.<br><br>Comments: |
| ☐ Yes<br>☐ No<br>☐ Not Sure | We have created our fundraising plan and defined the roles and responsibilities we will need staff to fill.<br><br>Comments: |
| ☐ Yes<br>☐ No<br>☐ Not Sure | If part of a large organization or institution, we have talked with the human resources department regarding our staffing needs and their recruitment processes.<br><br>Comments: |
| ☐ Yes<br>☐ No<br>☐ Not Sure | We have created a job description for each employee we need to hire.<br><br>Comments: |
| ☐ Yes<br>☐ No<br>☐ Not Sure | Our job descriptions include quantitative evaluation criterion.<br><br>Comments: |
| ☐ Yes<br>☐ No<br>☐ Not Sure | We provide our staff with training opportunities throughout the year.<br><br>Comments: |
| ☐ Yes<br>☐ No<br>☐ Not Sure | Our budget includes membership fees for staff participation in the Association of Fundraising Professionals, the Council for Advancement and Support of Education, and other associations, as appropriate.<br><br>Comments: |

| | DESCRIPTION |
|---|---|
| ☐ Yes<br>☐ No<br>☐ Not Sure | We provide entry-level staff with opportunities for professional growth and advancement. |
| | Comments: |
| ☐ Yes<br>☐ No<br>☐ Not Sure | Our hiring committee includes fundraising professionals from our community who can help ensure we are making the right hire. |
| | Comments: |

## What Next?

If you answered yes to all or most of the above questions, well done! Your organization recognizes the importance of investing in highly skilled staff. Going forward, ensure that staff members maintain well-organized records. Reports, databases, and correspondence should be saved on a shared computer server. Staff should be aware of one another's projects and duties and able to provide coverage when needed. This will help operations run smoothly, even during times of high activity, such as a capital campaign.

If the checklist revealed that your organization is struggling with staffing or is weak in a specific area, use this as an opportunity for improvement. If in doubt, go back to the basics: your fundraising plan. Make sure that your current staff is prepared to fill the roles identified in the plan, and if not, determine how to reassign duties or what new positions to create.

Honestly assess the abilities and strengths of your current staff, and look for ways your organization can help them succeed. Are employees uncertain of their responsibilities? Do they feel valued and supported by your organization? Do they believe they will advance within the institution? What additional training is needed? Now is the time to delve deep into the potential of your staff and to make any necessary adjustments.

**Notes:**

_____

_____

# CHAPTER 10

# Take Me to Your Leader

**Leadership**

***Identify top-caliber volunteer leadership.***

By now you may have guessed that we place a priority on leadership. We believe that taking the time to recruit top-quality fundraising leaders pays off.

If you are wondering where you will find such individuals, we suggest that you begin looking for volunteer leadership from within existing relationships, starting with your long-term donors and current major donors.

While it may take a considerable amount of time to identify, solicit, and engage your top fundraising leadership, you will find that these efforts will yield results. The alternative is staff-led fundraising. There are very few organizations that can hire all the fundraising talent they need. And even if they could, staff-led fundraising is distinctly different from volunteer-led efforts. No organization can purchase the impact of people talking with their peers and asking them to join them in supporting a cause they believe in. "People give to people" is a truism that should never be overlooked.

The time and effort it will take to raise funds is greatly reduced by having the right volunteers committed and ready to take action on behalf of a cause or institution they believe in. It is best to delay the public launch of your fundraising activities until the right leaders are identified and committed.

As you recruit your chair, be sure to share your fundraising plan with her. Give her time to review your plan so that she can determine if she has the time, connections, and willingness to help you achieve your fundraising goals. Ask her who she believes would be the best person for each of the areas in which you need to engage volunteers.

Your chair (or co-chairs) should be the person to identify those individuals she most wants to work with as she helps your organization achieve its fundraising goals. We strongly advocate against identifying people you want the chair to work with. Let her pick her team.

Here are the top three things to remember in regard to fundraising leadership:
1. Leadership is critical to the success of any fundraising effort.
2. Fundraising must be volunteer-driven, with strong, experienced leadership.
3. People give to people.

## Volunteer Leadership Checklist

The following is a list of things to consider as you evaluate who would best serve in a volunteer leadership capacity:

| | **DESCRIPTION** |
|---|---|
| ☐ Yes | Track record of leadership in local and regional fundraising campaigns. |
| ☐ No<br>☐ Not Sure | Comments: |
| ☐ Yes | Belief in the mission and goals of the institution. |
| ☐ No<br>☐ Not Sure | Comments: |
| ☐ Yes | Financial means to make a leadership-level gift. |
| ☐ No<br>☐ Not Sure | Comments: |
| ☐ Yes | Well respected in the local community. |
| ☐ No<br>☐ Not Sure | Comments: |

| | DESCRIPTION |
|---|---|
| ☐ Yes<br>☐ No<br>☐ Not Sure | People cannot say "no" when asked by this person.<br><br>Comments: |
| ☐ Yes<br>☐ No<br>☐ Not Sure | Able to benefit from the position of fundraising chair personally and/or professionally.<br><br>Comments: |
| ☐ Yes<br>☐ No<br>☐ Not Sure | Able to recruit top community leaders to take on high-level volunteer leadership positions.<br><br>Comments: |
| ☐ Yes<br>☐ No<br>☐ Not Sure | Able to allocate the necessary time to lead and manage the fundraising initiative.<br><br>Comments: |
| ☐ Yes<br>☐ No<br>☐ Not Sure | Able to provide pro-bono resources to enhance fundraising planning and implementation.<br><br>Comments: |
| ☐ Yes<br>☐ No<br>☐ Not Sure | Able to make the case for support to key segments of the community.<br><br>Comments: |
| ☐ Yes<br>☐ No<br>☐ Not Sure | Able to participate in weekly fundraising management meetings, or to send a qualified and empowered representative when unable to attend.<br><br>Comments: |
| ☐ Yes<br>☐ No<br>☐ Not Sure | Someone who hates to fail.<br><br>Comments: |

| | DESCRIPTION |
|---|---|
| ☐ Yes  ☐ No  ☐ Not Sure | Has a personal, professional, or civic connection to the institution. |
| | Comments: |
| ☐ Yes  ☐ No  ☐ Not Sure | Easily accessible to other leadership. |
| | Comments: |
| ☐ Yes  ☐ No  ☐ Not Sure | Willing to buy into and operate from a fundraising plan. Able to provide input and suggested modifications to meet personal leadership style. |
| | Comments: |

## What Next?

Use this checklist as a tool to assess and prioritize which potential leaders you wish to approach. Some of the assets on this list may be especially important to your organization; seek out individuals who are strongest in those areas. If your first-choice candidate declines to accept a leadership role, explore other ways for her to get or stay involved. You may also wish to solicit her suggestions for good alternative candidates.

If you are struggling to identify strong candidates, circulate this list among staff, volunteers, and board members. Ask them to suggest individuals whom they believe meet all or most of the criteria. Over time, seek to involve these potential leaders in your organization by inviting them to events, sending them marketing materials, and making personal appeals. Capitalize on any existing relationships between your team members and candidates. Investing time in this process will help bolster the caliber of your volunteers and cultivate new leaders.

**Three Actions I Will Take:**

1. _____

2. _____

3. _____

CHAPTER 11

# Procedural Guideposts

***Craft fundraising guidelines, policies, and procedures.***

 Most people who are engaged with a non-profit are there to meet a personal or business need. They are highly charged with emotion and a passion to do good. But sometimes in the midst of doing good there may be a tendency to sidestep best practices that build credibility. One way to ensure credibility is for the board to craft, approve, and implement fundraising guidelines, policies, and procedures. These should be clearly worded and should support the work of board members, volunteers, staff, and donors.

We advise our clients to take the time to identify the full spectrum of guidelines, policies, and procedures needed to support their fundraising efforts — before launching a campaign. Choosing to adopt policies on an "as needed" basis is choosing to be reactive instead of proactive. When policies and procedures are clearly communicated, the work of fundraising is made easier.

For example, if you do not have a pledge policy in place, it can be frustrating for a volunteer solicitor to learn that the three-year pledge she secured from a local business leader requires a signed pledge form. If she had known, she would have informed the donor at the time she solicited the pledge. Having to come back to secure a signed pledge form means reopening negotiations. It provides the donor with an opportunity to reconsider her giving. It sends the signal that your organization does not have its house in order. It can frustrate your volunteer solicitors who find the need to spend additional time on a "completed" solicitation.

Take the guesswork out of fundraising. Define your policies and procedures. If unusual circumstances arise, respond to them. But have the fundamentals in place and apply them consistently. Nothing can lose the goodwill of an investor or volunteer more quickly than a situation where the rules are changing constantly. Take time and work with your board, staff, volunteers, and donors to develop guidelines, policies, and procedures that are credible and in line with your mission and culture.

## How It Works

1. The development committee of the board is responsible for drafting guidelines, policies, and procedures. They can work with your development staff, with a consultant, or with Internet resources to craft these.
2. The documents should be brought to the full board for discussion and approval.
3. Once approved, the guidelines, policies, and procedures should be implemented by staff and referred to on an ongoing basis.

The following is a partial list of the types of guidelines, policies, and procedures that should be in place. The Association of Fundraising Professionals has detailed information on these available on its website. You may also want to confer with comparable organizations in your community — or in other parts of the country — for examples.

1. **Gift acceptance:** This policy will make clear the types of gifts that your institution will accept and those that it won't accept. For instance, some health organizations have policies that state they will not accept funding from tobacco or alcohol companies. Some advocacy organizations will not accept government funds. Some gift acceptance policies clarify the date by which gifts of stock must be sold; others provide guidelines for how gifts of property will be handled.

2.  **Pledge acceptance:** This policy will make clear the requirements for accepting pledges. For example, what type of documentation is required before your institution will carry a pledge on its books? What is the maximum pledge period? For example, can a donor make a pledge that will be paid over ten years, or is the maximum pledge period three years?

3.  **Gift/pledge documentation:** This policy defines the type of documentation the institution will keep on gifts and pledges and how long that information needs to be retained. For example, does your institution keep copies of all checks received? Do you retain a copy of the original signed pledge form?

4.  **Acceptance of life insurance policies:** This policy provides guidance on how and when the value of such policies are counted toward a fundraising goal.

5.  **Accounting/recognition of bequests:** This policy defines how bequests are recorded and accounted for. For example, will your year-end fundraising report include the value of a gift included in the will of a 22-year-old? How are bequests recognized?

6.  **Naming opportunities:** This policy defines the criteria for naming opportunities. It can include minimum amounts for naming opportunities, an actual list of those items available for naming opportunities, conditions upon which naming rights may be revoked, and whether or not all naming opportunity agreements require final approval by the board.

7.  **Acceptance of in-kind gifts:** This policy defines how non-cash gifts will be accounted for. It also defines what types of non-cash gifts your organization is willing to accept.

8.  **Donor bill of rights:** This was created by the Association of Fundraising Professionals and is upheld as a standard to be adopted by institutions and shared with donors and prospective donors. A copy is available online at www.afpnet.org.

9.  **Fundraising code of ethics:** This was created by the Association of Fundraising Professionals and is upheld as a standard for use by people and institutions engaged in fundraising. A copy is available online at www.afpnet.org.

# Fundraising Policies Checklist

Use this checklist as you are considering the state of your organization's fundraising policies.

| | DESCRIPTION |
|---|---|
| ☐ Yes<br>☐ No<br>☐ Not Sure | A gift acceptance policy has been created, reviewed, and approved by our board. |
| | Comments: |
| ☐ Yes<br>☐ No<br>☐ Not Sure | A pledge acceptance policy has been created, reviewed, and approved by our board. |
| | Comments: |
| ☐ Yes<br>☐ No<br>☐ Not Sure | A gift/pledge documentation policy has been created, reviewed, and approved by our board. |
| | Comments: |
| ☐ Yes<br>☐ No<br>☐ Not Sure | A policy that defines how we account for and recognize bequests has been created, reviewed, and approved by our board. |
| | Comments: |
| ☐ Yes<br>☐ No<br>☐ Not Sure | A naming opportunities policy has been created, reviewed, and approved by our board. |
| | Comments: |
| ☐ Yes<br>☐ No<br>☐ Not Sure | A policy that defines which in-kind gifts we will accept and how we will account for them has been created, reviewed, and approved by our board. |
| | Comments: |

| | DESCRIPTION |
|---|---|
| ☐ Yes<br>☐ No<br>☐ Not Sure | We have reviewed and approved the AFP Donor Bill of Rights as a policy for our institution. |
| | Comments: |
| ☐ Yes<br>☐ No<br>☐ Not Sure | We have reviewed and approved the AFP Fundraising Code of Ethics as a policy for our institution. |
| | Comments: |

## What Next?

If you are confident in your organization's fundraising policies, we commend you. Transparency is a necessary component of any effective organizational policy. Ensure your fundraising guidelines are communicated to all members of your organization and enforced consistently. As your organization grows or takes on new fundraising projects, keep your policies and procedures up to date and relevant.

If your organization's fundraising policies are lacking, or nonexistent, we urge you to address this problem before proceeding with any further fundraising efforts. Ask the board to prioritize the creation of a clear set of guidelines using the strategies and resources outlined above. These guidelines should be shared throughout your organization, and staff and volunteers asked to directly acknowledge their understanding and adherence. Without a firm set of rules governing the handling of donations, your organization risks alienating volunteers and donors and missing out on the full potential of their gifts.

**Notes:**_____

_____

_____


**Three Actions I Will Take:**

1. _____

2. _____

3. _____

CHAPTER 12

# Wanted: A Few Good Volunteers

***Recruit a team of properly trained and informed volunteers.***

An organization can never hire enough staff to ensure its fundraising success. And, even if it could, the case for support is often made most successfully by those who have given a gift themselves. These volunteers make the case in peer-to-peer solicitations. They are not asking because they are paid to but because they believe in the cause. Each volunteer's gift is used as an example and motivation for others to give. And, as noted earlier, long-term donors are excellent volunteers.

All volunteers should be recruited to fill specifically defined roles. The talent recruited should match the tasks to be fulfilled. When recruited, each prospective volunteer should be presented with a document detailing their roles, responsibilities, and the time frame of their commitment. Before they begin soliciting others, they need to make their own gift. Your volunteers should be solicited by the board chair or executive director in a way that will inspire the person to give both time and money. The solicitation of volunteers should model how the organization would like for them to solicit others.

Once recruited, volunteers should also be trained in general solicitation techniques and in how to make the case for your organization. Training should include role-playing in the processes of cultivation and solicitation.

The training should emphasize the organization's mission, purpose, and fundraising goals. It should instill a sense of urgency regarding fundraising that is consistently communicated to all volunteers.

This last point is of great importance, as each volunteer needs to be communicating the same message when she or he solicits a gift. There should be no confusion amongst prospective donors about why people are being asked to give and what the funds will be used for.

Once volunteers are trained and engaged in fundraising, they need to be constantly and consistently praised and recognized for their efforts. Volunteers can never be thanked enough. Their role is key and they need to be recognized throughout the duration of the fundraising initiative and beyond. Thanks and recognition can include special volunteer receptions/events, VIP treatment, consideration for a future board or policy-making position, and acknowledgement in all fundraising-related materials. It should be both personal and public.

## When A Volunteer Doesn't Fulfill Responsibilities

Should a situation arise where a volunteer is not fulfilling her roles and responsibilities, it is important for this situation to be addressed as quickly as possible. The fundraising chair should talk with the volunteer and inquire about any challenges the volunteer may be having and how these can be addressed. You may find that a person who originally believed she could fulfill your requests can no longer do so. Do not be dismayed. Find another, more appropriate way to retain the person and then begin the process of soliciting and training a new volunteer.

It is more important to have volunteers who fulfill their responsibilities than it is to have well-known people in place who are not advancing your fundraising goals.

# Volunteer Training Checklist

Use the following checklist to help you when training volunteers.

| | **DESCRIPTION** |
|---|---|
| ☐ Yes<br>☐ No<br>☐ Not Sure | Appropriate staff or board members have met with each volunteer and shared the organization's fundraising goals and reviewed (and, as appropriate, revised) expected roles and responsibilities.<br><br>Comments: |
| ☐ Yes<br>☐ No<br>☐ Not Sure | All volunteers have received a document defining their roles and responsibilities.<br><br>Comments: |
| ☐ Yes<br>☐ No<br>☐ Not Sure | A fundraising orientation workshop is held each year, or more often as necessary, to orient new staff, board members, and volunteers and to retain the engagement of those already involved.<br><br>Comments: |
| ☐ Yes<br>☐ No<br>☐ Not Sure | All volunteers have received a copy of our leadership handbook and current fundraising and marketing materials.<br><br>Comments: |
| ☐ Yes<br>☐ No<br>☐ Not Sure | Each volunteer is paired with a staff person or board member.<br><br>Comments: |
| ☐ Yes<br>☐ No<br>☐ Not Sure | Our financial goals and case for support are understood by all volunteers.<br><br>Comments: |

## Reminder

By definition, volunteers want to serve. Respect their time and talents by keeping them informed and engaged. If your organization's capacity for volunteers is temporarily reduced for any reason, let them know promptly. Assure them they are still needed, and keep in regular contact about upcoming assignments. Do not let any volunteer think he has been forgotten about or is unwanted, for he will direct his efforts elsewhere. Respond quickly to inquiries from new volunteers. If you do not have an immediate need for their assistance, get them involved in other ways. Never waste the good intentions of a volunteer committed to helping your organization achieve its goals.

Notes:_____

_____

_____

**Three Actions I Will Take:**

1. _____

2. _____

3. _____

## CHAPTER 13

# Technical Support

*Use a donor database system to facilitate fundraising management and decision making.*

Preparing for and implementing your fundraising plan will be facilitated through the use of your donor management software and database. If you don't already have such a system in place, we suggest you make this a goal with an achievable timeline. Start with a system that can support the level of simplicity or complexity present in your organization.

Fundraising activities and milestones need to be tracked and reported on. This will help your current initiative and will also help with future fundraising.

The following is a list of the types of activities that we recommend you track:
1. Donors
2. Events
3. Funds pledged
4. Funds received
5. Geographic location of donors
6. Lapsed donors
7. Outstanding pledge balances
8. Prospective donors
9. Prospective volunteers
10. Relationships between all parties ("who knows who")

11. Solicitations
12. Volunteers

The following is a list of the data elements we recommend that you track:
1.  Names, addresses, telephone numbers, and email addresses of current and prospective donors
2.  Names, addresses, telephone numbers, and email addresses of fundraising leadership and volunteers, and the division each is associated with
3.  Assigned solicitor and division for each prospective donor
4.  Target gift amount for each prospective donor
5.  Actual amount of gift or pledge
6.  Payments against pledges
7.  Acknowledgement and recognition received
8.  Notes and contact reports from visits and calls with current and prospective donors

The following is a list of the fundraising summary reports we recommend you produce and review on a monthly basis:
1.  Number of new prospects identified
2.  Total amount of gifts received for the month (number of gifts and dollar value)
3.  Total amount of pledges received for the month (number of pledges and dollar value)
4.  Total funds received and pledged to date (combined gifts and pledges)
5.  Percentage of fundraising goal achieved to date
6.  Total amount of funds received to date (exclude pledges)
7.  Total amount of pledge funds received and amount outstanding
8.  Lapsed pledges (show which donors are behind in fulfilling their pledges)

All contacts need to be recorded so that the organization's history with a donor can be known throughout the organization. "Contacts" include meetings, gifts, conversations, and attendance at special events. Too often the relationships between donors, prospects, and volunteers is not tracked and recorded, and when a key person leaves the organization, the information leaves with that person. Tracking this information ensures that all parties are on the organization's official mailing list, and that solicitation strategies have a full spectrum of relationship information to draw on.

**Note:** Recording the contacts made during today's fundraising provides information for future initiatives. You are creating organizational history and memory by recording information on who you meet with, who you mail to, who attends events, and who is identified as a prospective donor for your current initiative. This information will become part of the institution's backbone (institutional memory) and valuable to new staff. Given the high rate of employee turnover in many organizations and institutions, it is important to create and maintain a record of interactions with current and prospective donors along with information about their interests, relationships with other donors or staff, and philanthropic priorities.

# Tracking Activities And Progress

Accurate and up-to-date data is critical to properly monitoring and managing fundraising. It also helps build credibility amongst donors and the public and can assist fundraising leadership in making tactical decisions and readjustments necessary to ensure financial goals are met.

Take the time to review available donor management software. Unless absolutely necessary, we advise against creating your own software or database. These can be difficult to maintain if the developer leaves your organization. Commercially available software includes access to upgrades, technical support, and training. The Association of Fundraising Professionals evaluates software on a regular basis.

# Donor Management System Checklist

Use this checklist to assess your database management operations.

| | DESCRIPTION |
|---|---|
| ☐ Yes<br>☐ No<br>☐ Not Sure | We have easy-to-follow data entry procedures that are documented and updated regularly. |
| | Comments: |
| ☐ Yes<br>☐ No<br>☐ Not Sure | Our database tracks relationships between donors, staff, board members, volunteers, and others engaged with our organization. |
| | Comments: |

| | DESCRIPTION |
|---|---|
| ☐ Yes<br>☐ No<br>☐ Not Sure | Gifts and pledges are entered into the database within 24 hours of receipt. |
| | Comments: |
| ☐ Yes<br>☐ No<br>☐ Not Sure | We create donor profiles for our major donors that are stored in the database. |
| | Comments: |
| ☐ Yes<br>☐ No<br>☐ Not Sure | We update the contact information in our database on a monthly basis. |
| | Comments: |
| ☐ Yes<br>☐ No<br>☐ Not Sure | Our staff, board members, and fundraising volunteers submit contact reports for entry into the database after visiting with current/prospective donors and after meaningful phone calls or email exchanges. |
| | Comments: |
| ☐ Yes<br>☐ No<br>☐ Not Sure | The information for married couples is accurately recorded so that our emails are properly addressed and include both names. |
| | Comments: |
| ☐ Yes<br>☐ No<br>☐ Not Sure | We have identified the reports that need to be produced each month and have documented the procedures for how these are to be produced so that we are not dependent on any one person for this action. |
| | Comments: |

## Tip

No matter how "smart" a donor management system, humans provide the vital touch. Set clear expectations among staff for the consistent and correct use of your system. Staff must be fully trained and confident in the use of relevant software in order to effectively manage donor information. New employees should receive training promptly upon being hired, and all staff should undergo period review sessions. Make sure that operating procedures are well documented and accessible. System updates or procedural revisions should be communicated immediately across the organization.

**Notes:**_____

_____

_____

**Three Actions I Will Take:**

1. _____

2. _____

3. _____

CHAPTER 14

# Approaching Donors

***Coordinate solicitation strategies.***

Have you ever had the experience of asking someone to give a gift to an organization you are fundraising for only to find out that someone else has already talked with that person about giving? Or worse yet, have you asked a couple for a gift only to find out they made a meaningful gift last month?

Coordinated solicitation strategies can help avoid these situations and the negative impact that can be associated with such mistakes.

We recommend using your data management system to help coordinate your solicitation strategies. Here are some steps you can use:

1. Identify which donors you want to ensure are personally solicited.
2. For each donor, review information in your database to see who knows the donor or has a relationship with him/her.
3. If long-term or major donors do not have a solicitor associated with their donor records, here are some steps you can take to find and record information regarding solicitation:
    a. Ask others involved with your organization about who has been responsible for soliciting each donor in the past, and record that information. This is especially helpful if your institution is new to recording the diverse data and information that can help future

     fundraising initiatives. It is also useful if you have long-term leadership at the staff or board level who "keep everything in their head" — record this information so everyone can benefit from it in the future.

  b.  If you solicit funds nationally, run donor reports against your database by geographic area. This can provide you with information regarding who lives near your current or prospective donors. This can help you identify a prospective solicitor — someone who knows the person in question and/or would be willing to ask her for a gift.

4.  Create a list of the donors who should be personally solicited.

5.  Share your list of donors to be personally solicited with your board members, CEO, fundraising volunteers, alumni, and even other donors. Ideally, the list should be shared in personal one-on-one meetings during which you would ask questions such as:

  a.  Do you know any of the people on this list?

  b.  Do you know how they feel about our organization?

  c.  Do you think they would be interested in supporting our fundraising?

  d.  Who do you think is the best person to talk with the people you know?

Note: Be sure to record information in your database regarding donor relationships and interests.

6.  Ensure each donor is assigned to the person you and your fundraising leadership team believe is the "best" solicitor.

7.  Remember: Each person who solicits a gift should have already made his own gift.

When it's your turn to solicit a gift you can use the following suggestions as you prepare for and conduct your conversation. If you have not done this before, take some time to practice with a friend, co-worker or spouse.

1.  **Make your own gift first.** If you believe people should give to an organization, you need to demonstrate that by making your own gift. If you are not willing to give, why should someone else?

2.  **Make a personal visit.** Asking for a gift should be done in person whenever possible.

3.  **Be prepared.** Know the people you are soliciting. What are their interests? Why would they want to make a gift? How would their gift impact your institution?

4.  **Be prepared.** Bring information such as a brochure, photos, or copies of relevant articles. If a DVD is available, bring that.

5. **Make a brief and concise presentation.** Talk about your organization's history, current activities and vision for the future. Talk about what specifically you are raising money for and how the money will be used.
6. **Sell the unique value of your institution.** Use emotion as well as fact. Talk about what this institution means to you and why you are involved.
7. **Ask for a specific, reasonable and challenging gift.** Know the amount you will ask for. It shouldn't be too small an amount, nor too large.
8. **Bring a list of donor benefits.** Communicate how your institution honors and recognizes its donors. Review the tangible and intangible benefits offered to donors.
9. **Talk about the gift you made.** If your gift is similar to what you would like your prospect to give, state the amount you gave and why.
10. **MAKE THE ASK.** Be sure to specifically ask for a gift, "I would like for you to make a gift to the ABC organization. Would you be willing to contribute $___?"
11. **Pause after you ask for the gift.** Do not rush to fill the silence. Give the person time to respond, for they will.
12. When the person says YES, thank them and ask how they would like to make their gift.
13. If the person says NO, ask what would be the right amount at this time.
14. If the person says this is not the right time, ask what would be a good time.
15. Regardless of the outcome, thank the person for their time.
16. After each meeting, send a thank you note regardless of whether a gift was made.

## SOLICITATION STRATEGY CHECKLIST

Use the following solicitation strategy checklist as you review your list of current and prospective donors and determine the strategies that will work best.

| | DESCRIPTION |
|---|---|
| ☐ Yes<br>☐ No<br>☐ Not Sure | We have a defined strategy for each of our current and prospective donors (direct mail, event invitation, Internet communication, personal cultivation, solicitation, and stewardship). |
| | Comments: |

| | DESCRIPTION |
|---|---|
| ☐ Yes<br>☐ No<br>☐ Not Sure | Each donor has been assigned to a staff person and a volunteer for implementation of the defined strategy. |
| | Comments: |
| ☐ Yes<br>☐ No<br>☐ Not Sure | Assigned staff and volunteers help define the specifics of how current and prospective donors should be cultivated and solicited. |
| | Comments: |
| ☐ Yes<br>☐ No<br>☐ Not Sure | Timelines are associated with the cultivation and solicitation strategy for each donor. |
| | Comments: |
| ☐ Yes<br>☐ No<br>☐ Not Sure | Staff and volunteers are provided with training and role-playing opportunities to build their confidence in soliciting gifts. |
| | Comments: |
| ☐ Yes<br>☐ No<br>☐ Not Sure | Staff and volunteers report on the progress of their cultivation and solicitation work. |
| | Comments: |
| ☐ Yes<br>☐ No<br>☐ Not Sure | Direct mail, events, and Internet communications are coordinated to support each other and to support personal cultivation and solicitation activities. |
| | Comments: |

# Reminder

Relationships are vital to long-term giving. Cultivate donor relationships through consistency and quality in your outreach efforts. Highly valued donors or potential donors should not be made to interact with more than one or two fundraising contacts within your organization. This strategy allows your fundraising team to build trust with donors and to make solicitations that are personalized, carefully timed, and successful. An organized and dependable fundraising team encourages giving by demonstrating to donors that their contributions will be well managed and appropriately acknowledged.

**Notes:**_____

_____

_____

**Three Actions I Will Take:**

1. _____

2. _____

3. _____

CHAPTER 15

# Broadcast the Message

*Create a strong awareness and education program to complement and support fundraising activities.*

Fundraising requires the support of a well-orchestrated marketing program. If people do not know about your organization, there is little reason for them to give. Marketing creates awareness of your organization, its mission, values, vision, and goals. It makes the case for why people should give and it invites them to do so. When well designed, your marketing program will increase awareness of your organization and educate people about its important work.

It is very hard to promote giving to an organization that no one knows or that no one has emotional ties to. Your awareness and education program should communicate and promote the following aspects of your organization:
1. Vision
2. Values
3. Mission
4. Organizational goals
5. Case for support
6. Most importantly, your call to action

Clear and consistent communication with your defined constituency is a stepping-stone to meaningful results. Don't try to communicate with the whole world. Define your priority audiences and speak to them. Work with volunteers, staff, board members, and/or consultants who have the communications expertise you need. Develop a marketing plan that incorporates awareness, education, and fundraising. Make sure it is coordinated with your organization's fundraising plan. Most importantly, implement it.

# Awareness

The awareness phase of your marketing plan should focus on the following two priorities:
1. Creating general awareness for the organization, its strengths, and impact
2. Creating awareness for specific programs you are fundraising for without asking for financial support

Once 50–60 percent of your funds have been raised, the marketing focus should change to creating awareness for your fundraising. It should highlight initial donors/sponsors and funds raised. Materials should include a call to action and provide information on different ways to make a gift or get involved.

**Awareness activities should create visibility, excitement, and a desire to be involved** with the organization and — at the appropriate time — with its fundraising. These activities should be well planned and should tie to key fundraising milestones.

Awareness and marketing messages should be designed with care to ensure that investors, donors, organization members, and volunteers receive the same message from multiple sources, including:
1. Billboards
2. Blogs
3. Interviews
4. Newsletters (electronic and print)
5. Personal conversation
6. Print media
7. Public speeches
8. Radio
9. Social networking sites
10. TV (network and cable)
11. Twitter
12. Websites

Awareness activities will also need to include recognition of volunteer leadership and donors as well as updates on fundraising milestones. Because of this it is important that the institution's marketing team or committee work closely with the fundraising team. If consultants are hired for this role, they too need to work closely with the fundraising team.

Successful fundraising includes opportunities for donor and volunteer recognition. *Commitments made regarding public recognition will need to be fulfilled by the marketing and awareness team.*

## Education

Awareness activities often need to include an education element. As general awareness is created or increased, special care should be taken to educate the general public and key constituencies on specific aspects of your organization.

For example, if you provide job training opportunities, you will want to communicate what employment training needs exist within your community, the impact of unemployment or underemployment on individual families and the larger community, as well as potential barriers to employment and how these can be overcome. You may also want to educate your community and donors about the types of job training you offer, the length of each program, associated costs (if any), scholarships available, placement rates, employer partners, and the impact your programs make on families and the local economy.

Use the same communication methods for educating that you used to create awareness. Make it a point to communicate consistently and frequently. Remember the old marketing adage — it takes six impressions for a person to take action. You need to stay in front of your audience.

# Awareness And Education Checklist

Use this checklist as you review your organization's awareness and education activities.

| | DESCRIPTION |
|---|---|
| ☐ Yes<br>☐ No<br>☐ Not Sure | Our marketing and communications plan is up to date and is in sync with our fundraising plan. |
| | Comments: |
| ☐ Yes<br>☐ No<br>☐ Not Sure | Our marketing/communications staff and volunteers work closely with our fundraising staff and volunteers, sharing information, strategies, desired outcomes, and actual results. |
| | Comments: |
| ☐ Yes<br>☐ No<br>☐ Not Sure | We have produced an engaging and inspiring brochure. |
| | Comments: |
| ☐ Yes<br>☐ No<br>☐ Not Sure | Our website and blog communicate who we are, our impact, and how to give. |
| | Comments: |
| ☐ Yes<br>☐ No<br>☐ Not Sure | We have engaged professionals who give their time and talent to help create awareness and educate the public about our institution. |
| | Comments: |
| ☐ Yes<br>☐ No<br>☐ Not Sure | We provide our board members, donors, and volunteers with informational talking points they can use when blogging, writing letters to the editor, talking with their elected officials, or using Twitter. |
| | Comments: |

| | DESCRIPTION |
|---|---|
| ☐ Yes<br>☐ No<br>☐ Not Sure | We produce and distribute short videos for Internet circulation. |
| | Comments: |
| ☐ Yes<br>☐ No<br>☐ Not Sure | We produce short, current, and relevant press releases and distribute these in a timely fashion to relevant news outlets. |
| | Comments: |

## Tip

Feeling intimidated about using social media in your fundraising efforts? Take small, manageable steps. Begin by tasking one or two staff members or volunteers with exploring the best use of your online resources. Consider where you are most likely to reach your donors. For example, Twitter or text messages may hold greater appeal for young donors, while a blog or Facebook page may be more appropriate for older generations. Modify your messages accordingly — and keep them up to date! Do not launch social media accounts unless you have the staff to maintain them consistently and effectively. It is also vital to establish clear internal guidelines for social media activities. Delineate which staff members are authorized to use your organization's accounts and what type of content is appropriate to post. Establish a system of checks and balances to ensure your online presence accurately represents your organization and its fundraising goals.

Notes:_____

_____

_____

**Three Actions I Will Take:**

1. _____

2. _____

3. _____

**CHAPTER 16**

# Saying Thank You

***Thank and recognize donors and volunteers.***

People give to people, not to causes.

Appropriate recognition and appreciation is a great motivator for continued giving.

Too busy to say thank you? Don't have enough money in your budget to create a donor wall? When you realize how expensive it is to "save" on recognition and appreciation, you will change your tune.

It costs more to secure a new donor than it does to retain a current donor. Recognition, appreciation, and communication are the cornerstones of your donor recognition program.

The solicitation of a second gift begins as you recognize and appreciate a donor's first gift. The number-one task of development professionals and volunteer solicitors is to say thank you whether in person or by letter. After that you can offer an array of recognition opportunities, such as:

1. A donor wall
2. Certificates
3. Donor listings on your website
4. Invitations to VIP events
5. Leadership opportunities

6. Naming opportunities
7. Pins
8. Plaques
9. Public recognition in advertisements, brochures, and at events

Your recognition program should be integrated into your awareness and marketing program and should be understood by all members of your organization. Policies should be in place that clearly communicate the type of recognition that will accrue to individuals, businesses, and funders who provide financial support at specific levels. Your recognition program should be integrated with your donor benefits program (see chapter 17, starting on page 99) so that these two areas build on each other.

## Donor And Volunteer Recognition Checklist

Use this checklist to assess your donor and volunteer recognition program.

| | **DESCRIPTION** |
|---|---|
| ☐ Yes ☐ No ☐ Not Sure | There is one person assigned to ensuring a thank-you letter signed by the organization's president is mailed out within 48 hours of receipt of a gift. |
| | Comments: |
| ☐ Yes ☐ No ☐ Not Sure | Board members call donors who give major gifts to thank them. |
| | Comments: |
| ☐ Yes ☐ No ☐ Not Sure | When a volunteer solicits a gift, we let the solicitor know when a gift arrives so she too can thank the donor. |
| | Comments: |

| | DESCRIPTION |
|---|---|
| ☐ Yes<br>☐ No<br>☐ Not Sure | The names and contact information of all donors are entered into our database within 48 hours of receipt of a gift or an address update. |
| | Comments: |
| ☐ Yes<br>☐ No<br>☐ Not Sure | Our website includes a "Thank You" page that lists donors, sponsors and underwriters. It is updated each month. |
| | Comments: |
| ☐ Yes<br>☐ No<br>☐ Not Sure | If we have agreed to establish a donor wall, we add names to it each quarter. |
| | Comments: |
| ☐ Yes<br>☐ No<br>☐ Not Sure | We have identified which donors should be invited to all events as part of their donor benefit package and we make sure each one receives a special VIP invitation to attend for free. |
| | Comments: |
| ☐ Yes<br>☐ No<br>☐ Not Sure | We have written out the details of our donor and volunteer recognition program. |
| | Comments: |
| ☐ Yes<br>☐ No<br>☐ Not Sure | Our marketing and communications team has a copy of the donor and volunteer recognition program document and refer to it, ensuring that our benefits are incorporated into our marketing and communications efforts. |
| | Comments: |

Our fundraising team shares information regarding donors and volunteers with our marketing and communications team to ensure that everyone is included and that names are spelled correctly.

## What Next?

If you answered yes to most of the above items, we applaud your investment. Making the effort to recognize, track, thank, and follow up with donors leads to continued giving and support. Always value the time and resources of your donors. Be effusive with your thanks but proceed carefully when asking for the next donation. A heartfelt thank-you note followed up a week later by another request for funds may lead to donor fatigue and frustration. Use your donor database system to manage the appropriate timing of subsequent requests.

If your organization performed poorly on this checklist, investigate the problems and address them immediately. Is a breakdown in communication causing donations to go unreported in your database? Are your staff ill-prepared to write personalized thank-you notes? Are your recognition programs poorly defined? Donors whose contributions go unacknowledged will stop giving — not only because they feel underappreciated but because the organization appears unreliable. It is your goal to make donors feel secure in their giving by promptly and adequately thanking them for their support.

Notes:_____

_____

_____

**Three Actions I Will Take:**

1. _____

2. _____

3. _____

CHAPTER 17

# Giving Back

*Offer meaningful donor benefit packages and naming opportunities.*

Believe it or not, giving is part of a reciprocal relationship. As your donors give to you, so should you be prepared to give to them. And, you should be prepared to meet their unstated needs. A tall order? We think not. Just as you want to be on the top of your donors' minds as they make their giving decisions, so should your donors be on the top of your mind as you plan for the meaningful benefits you would like to offer.

The following are a few of the "needs" we have identified for you to consider as you create donor benefit packages for your donors. Each donor may have different needs.

1. The need for public recognition
2. The need to remain anonymous
3. The need to be identified with your organization for business or political purposes
4. The need to feel a part of a community
5. The need to be associated with like-minded people
6. The need to honor a family member, mentor, or public figure
7. The need to feel like a member of an exclusive group
8. The need to be recognized as a community leader

9.  The need to feel important
10. The need for social status
11. The need to give back
12. The need to make a difference
13. The need to meet new people
14. The need to grow one's business

Donor benefits should be packaged so that all people or organizations who give to your institution receive a baseline level of benefits. Be generous as you create these packages — don't be stingy. Make people feel good about giving. Let your donors feel that they are getting value from their giving.

Structure your benefits so that donors who could make a larger gift will consider stretching to a higher gift level in order to obtain the benefit package association with giving a larger gift.

Think about what makes your institution unique.

| UNIQUE FEATURE | RELATED BENEFIT YOU COULD OFFER |
|---|---|
| There is a distinct building on your campus that is locally or nationally recognized. | Photos or drawings of the building signed by the photographer or artist. Some could be framed. Offer larger and smaller sizes. |
| There is an award-winning scholar on your faculty. | Free tickets and VIP seating to an upcoming lecture. Opportunity to sit in on a class. |
| Your basketball team is on a winning streak. | Free tickets with VIP parking. |
| Your theater is known for attracting regional talent. | Free tickets and an opportunity to meet with actors after the show. |

| Unique Feature | Related Benefit You Could Offer |
|---|---|
| The attorneys who advocate for your cause are making headlines. | Invitation to lunch with the legal team to learn implications of success or failure. |
| Your hospital is the only one in the area offering cardiac care for children. | Invitation to tour the new children's cardiac care wing. |

Other benefits you may want to incorporate:
1. A special commemorative pin
2. Invitations to meet with the executive director or other leadership for intimate luncheons or breakfast meetings
3. Inclusion on a committee
4. Advertising in related publications. Offer black-and-white and color advertising in different sizes depending upon the gift level
5. Sponsorship of an upcoming event, including the opportunity to retain sponsorship level over a multi-year period
6. Invitation to give remarks or make introductions at special events
7. Opportunity to offer students (or your organization's clients or participants) internships
8. Naming opportunities, including naming of scholarships, buildings, rooms, programs, building wings, or events
9. Limited-edition caps, sweatshirts, or T-shirts
10. Access to a library or research center

Things to remember:
1. Make sure that your fundraising budget includes the costs associated with the benefits you are offering.
2. If your benefit packages include complimentary tickets to upcoming events, be sure to include those tickets in the planning and budgeting for the events so that special invitations are sent, tables are set aside, and the revenue is adjusted to reflect the complimentary tickets.

# Donor Benefit Checklist

Use this checklist to assess your donor benefit packages and policies.

| | DESCRIPTION |
|---|---|
| ☐ Yes<br>☐ No<br>☐ Not Sure | We have identified a core set of benefits that all donors will receive as a result of giving to our institution. |
| | Comments: |
| ☐ Yes<br>☐ No<br>☐ Not Sure | We have defined a series of giving levels at which additional benefits accrue. For example, $5,000, $15,000, $25,000. |
| | Comments: |
| ☐ Yes<br>☐ No<br>☐ Not Sure | There is one person in our office responsible for ensuring that donors receive the benefits associated with their giving level. |
| | Comments: |
| ☐ Yes<br>☐ No<br>☐ Not Sure | We have a policy in place that clarifies when donor benefits should be awarded for pledges — either at the time the pledge is made, upon fulfillment of the pledge, or at specific fulfillment milestones. |
| | Comments: |
| ☐ Yes<br>☐ No<br>☐ Not Sure | Our board has approved the naming opportunities associated with our benefit packages. |
| | Comments: |
| ☐ Yes<br>☐ No<br>☐ Not Sure | Donor benefits are promoted throughout our fundraising materials, including brochures and websites. |
| | Comments: |

| DESCRIPTION | |
|---|---|
| ☐ Yes<br><br>☐ No<br><br>☐ Not Sure | Our volunteers know and understand the different donor benefit packages we offer and know how to communicate them to prospective donors to help encourage higher levels of giving. |
| | Comments: |

## Reminder

Donors are unique, and so are their reasons for giving to your organization. Get creative when developing your donor benefit packages. Although these gifts may be little more than icing on the cake for a truly committed donor, they serve an important role as a memorable expression of gratitude. Ask each department or committee within your organization to suggest at least one truly innovative donor benefit package. Draw upon their insider perspectives: staff may have insights into lesser-known attributes of your institution; board members may be aware of the relevant hobbies of donors; volunteers may have ideas based upon their involvement with other community groups. Among your benefits, incorporate several options designed to surprise and delight. Even if they opt for a more traditional package, donors will appreciate your originality.

Notes:_____

_____

_____

**Three Actions I Will Take:**

1. _____

2. _____

3. _____

CHAPTER 18

# Talk It Out

*Encourage open lines of communication amongst all parties, combined with a sense of urgency.*

**Communication** It's all about communication.

Successful fundraising initiatives require the resources and expertise of a number of people such as board members, staff, volunteers, consultants, donors, granting agencies, and others. To keep all parties on the same page, it is paramount that clear and open lines of communication are in place. The Achilles' heel of a fundraising initiative is not being able to keep all parties informed.

We believe you have to make the case — constantly — both internally and externally. You need to communicate clearly and consistently to the people who are involved with your fundraising and with your current and prospective funders. You have to plan in advance so that getting the word out in a clear, concise, and compelling manner is part of your fund development culture. Failure to communicate well leads to confusion, suspicion, and apathy.

Fundraising can be very complex, detailed, and emotional. It is very easy to create confusion, bad feelings, and misinformation. These are the nightmares of fundraising that, if big enough, can take years to overcome. It is a public relations nightmare when you have staff and volunteers operating without knowledge of what the other is doing or saying. When conflicting information begins to circulate, the situation is even harder to manage and more time-consuming.

# It's Urgent!

We cannot understate the importance of communicating a sense of urgency. Fundraising is a competitive endeavor. If you are running an annual fundraising campaign, there is a lot to do each year. There are schedules to be met and activities that require advance work. Donors typically don't make a gift after their first interaction with an organization. You can't have a second visit until you've had the first. And don't forget, the summer is a hard time to engage people due to vacations and/or kids' being out of school. Another challenging time is mid-November to mid-January. Unfortunately, you don't have 12 months out of the year to advance your fundraising.

# Communication Checklist

Creating a system to ensure open lines of communication should be high on your list of priorities. Use the following as you move forward in this area.

| | DESCRIPTION |
|---|---|
| ☐ Yes | Information is shared freely on a timely basis. |
| ☐ No ☐ Not Sure | Comments: |
| ☐ Yes | Notes from meetings are shared with participants and those who need to know within 24 hours. |
| ☐ No ☐ Not Sure | Comments: |
| ☐ Yes | All volunteers, board members, and staff receive regular updates regarding fundraising activities and milestones. |
| ☐ No ☐ Not Sure | Comments: |
| ☐ Yes | Our fundraising team meets monthly to share progress, updates, and strategies. |
| ☐ No ☐ Not Sure | Comments: |

| | DESCRIPTION |
|---|---|
| ☐ Yes<br>☐ No<br>☐ Not Sure | The CEO is accessible to the chief fundraising officer and others. She shares information regarding strategic directions, new programs, and operations so the fundraising team remains informed. |
| | Comments: |
| ☐ Yes<br>☐ No<br>☐ Not Sure | Anyone can ask a question and receive an answer. |
| | Comments: |
| ☐ Yes<br>☐ No<br>☐ Not Sure | Our donor files are up to date and available for the donor to review if he requests to see his file. |
| | Comments: |
| ☐ Yes<br>☐ No<br>☐ Not Sure | We thank our donors for their gifts and pledges within 48 hours of receiving a gift. |
| | Comments: |
| ☐ Yes<br>☐ No<br>☐ Not Sure | All phone calls are returned with 24 hours. |
| | Comments: |
| ☐ Yes<br>☐ No<br>☐ Not Sure | Everyone who calls our office is treated as a VIP. All callers are treated with the respect and responsiveness. |
| | Comments: |
| ☐ Yes<br>☐ No<br>☐ Not Sure | All email communications include complete contact information so staff can be easily contacted. |
| | Comments: |
| ☐ Yes<br>☐ No<br>☐ Not Sure | Our website is up-to-date with current content. |
| | Comments: |

| | DESCRIPTION |
|---|---|
| ☐ Yes<br>☐ No<br>☐ Not Sure | Our e-marketing program is consistent, content-rich and donor-focused. |
| | Comments: |

## Tip

Team members tend to communicate well when working toward common goals. Avoid creating competition among staff, volunteers, board members, and executive leadership. A more productive strategy is to incentivize collaboration. This can be achieved in part by ensuring that all team members understand and embrace their responsibilities and recognize the role their efforts play in the overall success of the organization. Set clear protocols for internal and external communication and for data collection and reporting practices, emphasizing that the actions of each individual contribute to organizational efficiency and longevity. Inspire team members to never lose sight of their mission, and to support one another in achieving it.

**Notes:**_____

_____

_____

**Three Actions I Will Take:**

1. _____

2. _____

3. _____

# Go For It!

Fundraising is all about planning — planning, planning, and more planning. The truth is that very little time is actually spent asking people for money. As we write in our first book, *The Fundraiser's Guide to Soliciting Gifts: Turning Prospects into Donors*, fundraising is 90 percent preparation.

This document has outlined 18 prerequisites for fundraising success. While there are no shortcuts, following these suggestions will ensure a strong foundation for your fundraising efforts. These prerequisites are designed to help you build your organization's fundraising infrastructure and capacity. You will find that as you put these in place you will be changing the culture of your organization. You will be moving toward volunteer-driven fundraising. You will be increasing the level of accountability and transparency within your organization. You will be providing volunteers with an opportunity to give of their strengths in ways that are meaningful for them. Regardless of your size, you will find that you are becoming more community-based and more inclusive.

Choosing to shortcut these steps can imperil your fundraising and your organization.

Successful fundraising creates wonderful public relations opportunities and goodwill. It invigorates volunteers and positions the organization as successful and able to implement its vision. People like to give time and money to an organization that has proven itself and that has a reputation as a winner. Your fundraising decisions should be made based on a realistic assessment of whether or not financial, volunteer, and in-kind resources are available and can be sustained.

The lessons we have shared are based on years of experience. They have been tried and tested and are presented to help other organizations avoid mistakes that can be damaging in both the short term and long term. They are lessons that can help any non-profit organization. They will help you both raise money and transform your organization. Truly, they are prerequisites for fundraising success, and so much more.

# About the Authors

Melvin B. Shaw offers more than 40 years of experience in fund development and marketing. Formerly the vice president of marketing for the United Negro College Fund (UNCF), he created and produced the Lou Rawls Telethon, raising $4 million annually in corporate sponsorships and more than $500 million in annual gifts to date. Mel also served as the executive director of the Texas Association of Developing Colleges, facilitating joint programs and fundraising. He is nationally recognized for his work in creating and designing programs that combine marketing and fundraising and increase revenue and alumni/volunteer engagement. Mel's strategies create involvement and opportunities for corporate partnerships. He has developed cause marketing programs for Anheuser-Busch, General Motors, American Airlines, Chrysler Black Dealers Association, McDonald's, Essence Magazine, Disney World, and 7-Eleven.

Prior to forming Saad & Shaw Comprehensive Fund Development Services, he headed his own firm, Shaw & Company, which specialized in capital campaigns, annual giving, development assessments, feasibility studies, board development, campaign designs and planning, and major donors. Mel holds a Bachelor of Science degree from Lane College in Tennessee; a master's degree in business education from the University of Memphis; and was a fellow at Harvard University's Institute of Educational Management. In 1991 Mel received an honorary doctor of humanities degree from Lane College in recognition of his unique donor engagement and cause marketing programs and their impact on the fields of philanthropy and higher education.

Pearl D. Shaw, CFRE, is a fund development strategist and technical writer with management experience in the private and non-profit sectors. She has served as development director of the Women's Funding Network, an association of 100-plus women and girls' foundations, and as a major gifts officer for Mills College. Her private sector experience includes business development and marketing. Prior to forming Saad & Shaw Comprehensive Fund Development Services, she headed her own firm, Phrased Write, providing non-profit organizations with proposal writing, executive coaching, and strategic fund development services including major gifts work. Proposals she wrote secured a combined $6 million for clients such as the Omega Boys Club, Regional Technical Training Center, Centro de Servicios, Bay Area Black United Fund, and American-Arab Anti-Discrimination Committee, San Francisco.

As the principal writer for Saad & Shaw, Pearl writes the weekly column FUNdraising Good Times and is the co-author, with Melvin Shaw, of the book *The Fundraiser's Guide to Soliciting Gifts: Turning Prospects into Donors*. Pearl served as a member of the board of directors of the Development Executives Roundtable from 2002 to 2008, and is a member of the Association of Fundraising Professionals. She holds a Bachelor of Arts degree from the University of California at Berkeley, a master's degree in public administration from California State University East Bay, and is a certified fundraising executive.

# About Saad & Shaw

Saad & Shaw provides clients with a unique brand of fundraising that combines marketing, corporate partnerships, and the best of business leadership with fundraising fundamentals. The firm is known for designing innovative fundraising programs that increase revenue, strengthen partnerships, and provide value to all parties. Core services include campaign research, planning, design, and implementation. Clients include colleges and universities, health care institutions, grassroots groups, and philanthropy organizations.

The concepts and strategies employed by Saad & Shaw are based on the 50 years combined experience of principals Melvin and Pearl Shaw. In 2008 the Ford Foundation asked Mel and Pearl to share their unique brand of fundraising with social justice foundations from around the world at a conference held in Cartagena, Columbia, in South America. Saad & Shaw are proud to offer one of the most experienced, innovative, and creative powerhouse partnerships in fundraising consultancy today.

## counselOnDEMAND

Let Saad & Shaw help you meet your fundraising challenges and manage your fund development resources and staff effectively. The firm's counselOnDEMAND service provides flexible, low-cost fund development coaching and strategy sessions for executives and development directors. Clients receive five hours of on-call expertise each month. This service can be used for proposal and document reviews, strategy sessions, coaching and mentoring, the development of a fundraising plan, and more. counselOnDEMAND is ideal for organizations with limited budgets. For others it can be the first step in preparing for a feasibility study, the creation of a campaign plan, or as a follow-up service for continuing clients. Contact Saad & Shaw by emailing info@saadandshaw.com or calling (901) 522-8727 (Memphis) or (510) 798-4888 (Oakland).

## Learn More

To learn more about Saad & Shaw, including services, tips, and testimonials, visit www.saadandshaw.com.

Read Saad & Shaw's FUNdraising Good Times blog at fundraisinggoodtimes. com.

Made in the USA
Lexington, KY
02 February 2014